JOKES
FOR
TELLING

JOKES
FOR
TELLING

by

Kevin Goldstein-Jackson

PAPERFRONTS

ELLIOT RIGHT WAY BOOKS

KINGSWOOD, SURREY, U.K.

Printed and bound in Great Britain by Cox & Wyman Ltd, Reading, Berkshire.

Contents

Dedication

This book is dedicated to my two daughters, Sing Yu and Kimberley, and to thank Sing Yu (aged 4) for the joke she wanted me to include in this book and which she insisted on telling me every day for three months: Two biscuits were walking along the road. One got run over. What did the other one say? 'Oh, crumbs!'

It is also dedicated to my wife, Mei Leng, who knows all my jokes backwards – and frequently tells them that way!

Introduction

I was asked to write this book after readers had found my earlier books difficult to put down (they had been coated with invisible glue). It was also something to do after I'd made a killing on the Stock Market (I shot my broker); and was thinking of buying a newspaper shop (but it blew away) and an army surplus shop (but no one wanted to buy a surplus army). It also helped me recover from certain aspects of my childhood. For example, when I was a baby my parents gave me a rattle. I didn't much like it as whenever I picked it up the snake at the other end bit me.

As soon as people became aware that I was writing another joke book, apart from almost unanimous cries of 'Oh, no!' many people have given me jokes for inclusion in it – from friends (all two of them) to doctors, decorators and acquaintances.

Writing this book has certainly been good therapy to cheer myself up, and I hope it will do the same for you.

Some of the jokes you may well have heard of before, but I hope you will find a good number of them new, fresh and amusing: although some (particularly those based on puns) are intended to make you groan!

The jokes have been listed alphabetically under various subject headings, although sometimes it has been almost impossible to decide under which of several equally appropriate main headings a joke should appear.

In the interests of equality, there is a section of 'husband' jokes.

If you are using this book as a source of humour for speeches, then please select the jokes most appropriate for your intended audience. For example, certain people – if told a joke with a double-meaning – will fail to get either of them! And someone once defined tact as the ability to see others as they see themselves. Some jokes in this book are extremely old – but, then, nostalgia, too, is a thing of the past and yet many people still wallow happily in it. But it would be better to tell the older jokes to a younger audience which may not have heard them before.

Personally, I am a good judge of men in the audience. I can usually tell a man from a woman quite easily.

It is also important to remember that the best speeches are short. Indeed, the best after-dinner speech consists of only five words. This is when someone other than yourself says: 'Please give me the bill.'

If you stumble or stutter while making a speech, say something like: 'I knew I shouldn't have got these teeth by mail order.'

Finally, if you want to know my own favourite joke in this book – although it may make you groan – it's the joke about huskies under 'Romance.'

KG-J

Directory to the Book

On this, and the following 14 pages, is the directory to the 635 jokes in this book. So if you are reading the book for fun and are not searching for any particular subject, then skip all these pages and start on page 27.

The numbers given below refer to the number of the joke and *not* to the page number.

Happy joking!

JOKES

A

ACCIDENTS
1. Mr. Smith was just crossing a road on a zebra crossing when a car came hurtling towards him and, although he tried to jump out of the way, the car still managed to hit his side causing him to be thrown to the ground. A loud cackling noise could be heard from the car as it sped away.

A policeman who had witnessed the accident rushed up to Mr. Smith and asked: 'Did you see the driver? Or remember the car's registration number?'

'I didn't need to,' replied Mr. Smith. 'It was my wife who did it.'

'How do you know?' asked the policeman.

'Simple!' replied Mr. Smith. 'I'd recognise that hideous laugh anywhere.'

ACOUSTICS
2. The acoustics in the new theatre were so good the actors could hear every cough, whisper, crackle of sweet wrappers . . .

ACROBATS
3. I once knew two acrobats who fell head over heels in love.

ACTORS
4. Andrea: 'Dorothy, I can't understand why you still live with that dreadful actor friend of yours. You admit that he was rude to you at the party last night, and he's not even a good actor!'

Dorothy: 'I know. But I can't bring myself to bite the ham that feeds me.'

5. The Hollywood actor's career was on the decline and he seemed to spend all his time 'testing' for parts he never got, or trying to be seen in the right places and at the right parties in the hope of impressing some film mogul. Yet throughout this lean period in his career he remained hopeful that an upturn would soon come and he would be on his way to stardom.

It was in this state of mind that he returned home from his latest 'test' and was appalled to discover that his apartment had been totally wrecked. Paintings had been pulled from the walls and jumped on; a fire extinguisher had been sprayed all over the furniture and curtains; all the bottles in the bar area had been smashed; and in the middle of it all sat his girlfriend with blood pouring from her nose and with all the signs of having been involved in a fierce struggle.

'Who was it?' demanded the actor. 'I'll kill him!'

'Darling,' sobbed the girlfriend. 'It . . . it was the drink that must have made him do it. He arrived here totally drunk and went beserk the minute I let him in. It . . . it was your agent.'

'Why didn't you say so as soon as I got here, instead of sitting sobbing and bleeding like that?' demanded the actor. 'It must have been important for him to have come visiting my apartment. Did he leave a message?'

6. A friend of mine knew his son was going to be an actor when he caught him opening the 'fridge and taking a bow when the little light came on.

7. When Herbert auditioned to play the part of one of the seven dwarfs the director told him that he'd made the short list.

8. Theodore was so keen to get the part of Long John Silver in a new film that he actually had his leg amputated. Unfortunately he was turned down as he'd had the wrong leg off.

9. Conceited actor: 'I've practised my art with diligence and talent for so many years now that there is nothing I

cannot express simply by using my remarkably expressive face and without using mere words at all.'

Long-suffering friend: 'Well, can you express in your face alone – and without using any words – the following: you are an eighteen-year old man who is working down a coal mine and you have just heard – simultaneously – that you have won a fortune on the football pools and that your girlfriend, whom you love deeply, has been killed in a road accident by your brother whom you also love dearly and your mother has run off with the milkman and the coal mine is about to cave in?'

10. The ageing actor was trying to chat up the gorgeous young girl.

'Don't you recognise me?' he asked. She shook her head.

'But I'm quite well known in the movies,' he continued.

'Oh!' she said, her eyes lighting up. 'Where do you usually sit?'

ACTRESSES

11. Two ageing film actresses were walking along when one said: 'Do you know the best way to keep your youth?' The other replied: 'Lock him in the bedroom.'

12. I once knew the twenty-year old daughter of a Hollywood film actress who kept getting depressed because she didn't look as young as her mother.

13. Ever since the novice actress was told by the big movie producer that she had a nice profile she's walked around sideways.

14. The Hollywood film actress was getting married for the seventh time when the clergyman stumbled over the words of the ceremony.

'It's all right,' hissed the actress. 'Take it again from the top of page five.'

ADOLESCENCE
15. Adolescence is the period in life between puberty and adultery.

ADULTS
16. Adults are people who have stopped growing at the ends but have started to grow in the middle.

ADVICE
17. John: 'I just don't know what to do. What would *you* do if you were in my shoes?'

Alan: 'Polish them.'

AEROPLANES
18. Customer: 'A return ticket, please.'

Airline reservations clerk: 'Where to, sir?'

Customer: 'Back here, please.'

19. Very rich (but old) husband: 'I'm going to fire my pilot. He nearly killed me again today with his dreadful flying.'

Very young (but bored) wife: 'But, darling, can't you give him one last chance?'

20. Ethel: 'Excuse me, but I've heard that this 'plane travels faster than the speed of sound. Is that right?'

Air stewardess: 'Yes, madam, that's right. The Concorde certainly flies that fast.'

Ethel: 'But will it slow down at times so that I can talk to my companion and she can hear me?'

21. Air traffic controller: 'What is your height and position?'

Pilot: 'I'm about five feet ten inches tall and I'm sitting in the pilot's seat.'

22. Pilot: 'What's happened to all my controls? Some idiot has daubed black and white paint all over them!'

Trainee pilot: 'But you just told me to *check* the instrument panel, sir.'

AGE

23. My girlfriend says she is 'pushing thirty' – but slapped my face when I asked her from which direction.

ALARM CLOCK

24. Albert: 'I threw my alarm clock away this morning.'
John: 'Why?'
Albert: 'It kept going off when I was asleep.'

ANGLING

25. Fred: 'The fishing today wasn't very good.'
Claude: 'But I thought you'd had fifty bites?'
Fred: 'So I did: one small fish and forty-nine mosquitoes.'

26. 1st fisherman: 'Is this a good river for fish?'
2nd fisherman: 'Yes. It's so good that none of them are willing to leave it.'

27. A man walked into a fishmonger's and asked to buy six trout.

'Certainly, sir!' said the fishmonger, selecting the trout. He was about to wrap them up when the man said: 'No! Please don't wrap them up yet. Can you just gently throw them to me one by one?'

'I can,' replied the fishmonger. 'But why?'

'Well,' responded the man. 'I've been fishing all night and haven't caught anything. At least if you throw those trout to me and I catch them I can honestly say when I get home that I've caught six trout.'

28. John: 'Why are you fishing under that bridge in the pouring rain?'
Brian: 'Because that's where the fish will go to shelter.'

29. 'I'm never taking my sister fishing again,' sighed the small boy to his mother.

'Why not?' asked his mother. 'I know she's only two but the water isn't very deep and you can swim, so what's the problem?'

'She keeps eating all my maggots and worms.'

ANTI-SMOKING
30. The strong anti-smoker put a notice on the front door of his house stating: 'Abandon smoke all ye who enter here.'

ANTIQUES
31. Joan: 'Did you know I collect antiques?'
   Erica: 'Yes – I've seen your husband.'

APPLES
32. Sally: 'Mummy, do you like baked apples?'
   Mother: 'Yes, of course. Don't you remember, we had them last week. Why do you ask?'
   Sally: 'Because the orchard is on fire.'

ARISTOCRACY
33. The party of American hog slaughterers had been touring London for several days, visiting all the sights and being accompanied by various tour guides.
   'Tell me,' said one of the Americans to a tour guide, 'what's this "aristocracy" that you keep talking about. Who or what are they?'
   'Aristocracy,' replied the guide, 'is a collective noun used to describe a group of people who owe their position to their parents who, in turn, owe it to theirs and so on. The position is such that they need not do much and generally lead a life of leisure without having to bother much about earning money by hard work.'
   'Oh!' said the American who had asked the question. 'We have people like that in the U.S.A. too, only we call them tramps or hoboes.'

ASTROLOGERS
34. Two astrologers met each other in the street on a particularly cold and bitter day.

'Terrible winter we're having,' muttered one of the astrologers.

'Yes,' replied the other. 'It reminds me of the winter of 2057.'

AUTHORS

35. The famous author was boasting at a cocktail party: 'My last novel took three years to research and another year to write.'

Cocktail guest: 'What a waste of time. You could have bought one for about £2.50.'

36. His books are so bad they sell about as well as pork sausages in a synagogue.

B

BABIES

37. Sarah was walking along pushing her new baby in its pram when an old friend approached, looked into the pram and said: 'My, he's beautiful. He looks just like his father.'

'I know,' said Sarah. 'It's a pity he doesn't look more like my husband.'

38. Theobald: 'Darling, I know you're pregnant and that pregnant women often get strange cravings. But do you really have to eat so many old rubber tyres?'

Sandra: 'But I'm only trying to make sure we have a bouncing baby . . .'

39. Mr. and Mrs. O'Reilly had been trying for a son for many, many years and, after eleven daughters they were eventually rewarded with a son.

'Who does he look like?' asked a friend, visiting the maternity hospital to see Mrs. O'Reilly.

'We don't know,' replied Mrs. O'Reilly. 'We haven't looked at his face yet.'

40. The proud mother was showing off her new baby to her friend. 'Doesn't he look just like his father?' asked the mother.

'Yes,' replied the friend. 'But I shouldn't worry too much – he'll probably change for the better as he gets older.'

41. 'Ah,' said Mrs. Bigginswhistle, peering into the pram at her friend's baby. 'He looks just like his father – lying there on his back clutching a bottle.'

42. The elderly aunt bent down and asked her three year old nephew: 'Can you tell me the name of your new baby sister?'

The little boy shook his head sadly and replied: 'I don't know what it is. I keep asking her but I can't understand a word she says.'

BANK ACCOUNTS

43. Bank manager: 'And what sort of account would you like to open, Mr. and Mrs. Smith?'

Mrs. Smith: 'A joint account: Mr. Smith deposits and I draw out.'

BARBADOS

44. Resident of Barbados: 'In Barbados we always have fantastic weather.'

Visiting English woman: 'Then how on earth do you start a conversation with a stranger?'

BARBER

45. Claude (looking at his barber's bill): 'What? Ten pounds just to cut my hair – but I'm nearly bald . . .'

Barber: 'I know, sir. My charge is one pound for cutting the hair and nine pounds for search fees.'

BEARDS

46. Claude: 'Is it true that your rich aunt forced you to grow a beard?'

Derek: 'Yes. She will insist on buying me neckties.'

BED

47. Trying to persuade a baby to go to bed is hardest when she's beautiful and about eighteen years old.

BEDTIME STORIES

48. The liberated father was telling his small son a bedtime story: 'And in those olden times there were lots of wicked dragons about – large creatures which snorted fire from their nostrils. One day, one of these creatures captured the beautiful daughter of the King.

But there was a brave and bold knight who, on hearing of the plight of the princess, rapidly donned his armour and galloped off on his horse to rescue her.

After a long and bloody battle, the knight finally slayed the dragon and rescued the princess and took her back to the King's castle.

"You have done excellent work, knight, and have demonstrated your bravery and courage to the whole nation. I should be proud if you would take my daughter's hand in marriage – or become the husband of any of my other offspring."

Now, son, think carefully. Whom do you think the knight married?'

'The princess he rescued, of course,' replied the small son.

'No, you're wrong,' said the father. 'He married the King's son. After all, what else can you expect in a fairy story?'

BEES

49. The only reason bees buzz is because they can't whistle.

BEGGARS

50. Mr. Smith was taking his five-year old son for a walk when a beggar came up to him and said: 'Can you help me, sir? I haven't had a bite for a whole week.'

Before Mr. Smith could say anything, his son had bitten the beggar.

51. It is easy for a beggar to tell the difference between a politician and an accountant. If he asks a man for money for a meal saying he hasn't eaten all day, and the man replies: 'Sorry, no. But things will be better for you tomorrow.' That man must be a politician.

If the beggar asks the same question and a man replies: 'Sorry, no. But I'm interested to know how your financial situation compares with the same period last month' – then that man must be an accountant.

BIBLE
52. Five-year-old Clarence: 'Grandma, why do you always read the Bible for several hours every evening?'

Grandmother: 'Because I'm swotting for my finals.'

BIGAMY
53. Judge: 'You have been found not guilty of bigamy, so you can now be released and go home.'

Prisoner: 'Which home should I go to?'

BIG GAME HUNTING
54. Simon: 'That's a lovely stuffed bear you've got in your hallway.'

Colonel Bloggis: 'Thank you. I shot that when I went to Alaska hunting with old Bill Bloggett-Sykes.'

Simon: 'What's the bear stuffed with?'

Colonel Bloggis: 'Old Bill Bloggett-Sykes.'

BIRTHDAYS
55. Samantha: 'Do you know when Fred's birthday is?'

Sally: 'No. But I think it's sometime this year.'

56. I know a family that is so poor the parents couldn't afford to celebrate their son's eighteenth birthday until he was forty-nine.

57. My wife's best friend has just celebrated the twentieth anniversary of her twenty-ninth birthday.

BLOOD TESTS
58. She's so stupid she spent hours in the library trying to study for her blood test.

BOASTING
59. John was always boasting. In fact, he was probably the biggest boaster in the world – and the most conceited. He was also incredibly fat and must have weighed at least twenty-five stone.

People were therefore surprised when John died and his coffin appeared to be extremely small.

'Is that really John in there?' asked one of the people at the funeral.

'Of course!' was the reply. 'When all the wind was let out of him he only needed a small coffin.'

BODY BUILDING
60. My aunt Gladys took up body building recently. She did it so well that now she's my uncle.

BOOKS
61. *How To Juggle With Empty Beer Bottles* by Beatrix.

62. *Twenty-six Letters in Order* by Alf A. Bett.

63. *How To Tame Lions* by Claude Bottom.

64. *Bull Fighting* by Matt A. Dore.

65. *How To Improve Your Memory* by Ivor Gott.

66. *Pass The Sick Bags* by Eve Itt-Upp.

67. *Panties Fall Down* by Lucy Lastic.

68. *Highwaymen Through The Ages* by Stan Dan D. Liver.

69. *Not Quite The Truth* by Liza Lott.

70. *Sleepless Nights Together* by Constance Norah.

71. *The Naughty Boy* by U.R.A. Payne.

72. *Uncertainty* by R.U. Shore.

73. *Deathly Cookery* by R. Snick.

74. *Very Old Furniture* by Anne Teak.

75. *Want A Kiss?* by Miss L. Toh.

76. *Singing Between Tenor and Bass* by Barry Tone.

77. *How To Grow Squashy Red Fruit* by Tom. R. Tow.

78. *How To Win* by Vic Tree.

79. *Carpet Fitting For All* by Walter Wall.

BOOKSHOPS

80. Customer: 'I'd like to buy a novel, please.'

Bookshop assistant: 'Certainly, madam. Do you have the title or name of the author?'

Customer: 'Not really. I was hoping you could suggest something suitable that I could read.'

Bookshop assistant: 'No problem. Do you like light or heavy reading?'

Customer: 'It doesn't matter. I've left the car just outside the shop.'

BORROWERS

81. There was a knock on the door. Mr. Jones sighed and said to his wife: 'I bet it's that Bloggis fellow from next door wanting to borrow something else. He's already borrowed half the things in our house!'

'I know, dear,' replied Mrs. Jones. 'But why do you have to give in to him every time? Why not make some excuse so he can't borrow whatever he's come to borrow?'

'Good idea!' agreed Mr. Jones and he went and opened the door to Bloggis.

'Good morning,' said Bloggis. 'I'm sorry to trouble you, but I wondered if you would be using your garden shears this afternoon?'

'I'm afraid I will,' responded Mr. Jones. 'In fact, my wife

and I will be spending the whole afternoon gardening.'

'That's what I thought,' said Mr. Bloggis. 'Now I know you'll be too busy to use your golf clubs so perhaps you won't mind if I borrow them.'

BOSSES

82. Office junior: 'Please sir, can I have a day off next month?'

Boss: 'What for?'

Office junior: 'I'm getting married.'

Boss: 'But you only earn thirty pounds a week; you look like a tramp; and you've no hope of ever rising above being an office junior. What sort of idiot would marry you?'

Office junior: 'Your daughter, sir.'

83. Sally: 'You have to admire the boss in my office.'

Samantha: 'Why?'

Sally: 'If you don't he demotes you to post-room messenger.'

84. Cyril: 'Do you still work for the same boss?'

Clifford: 'Yes – the wife and two kids.'

85. Employee: 'Please, sir, can I have a day off work next month?'

Boss: 'A day off next month! A day off next month! Whatever next! After all I've done for you over the past thirty years. Reasonable wages. You've never been ill so you've always enjoyed your annual week's holiday. And after all that you ask for a day off next month! Do I have to tolerate such idiotic requests *every* thirty years?'

86. Everyone has a good word for our boss – but we have to whisper it behind his back.

87. Office manager: 'Sir?'

Boss: 'Yes? What is it now?'

Office manager: 'Please can I have a day off next week to do some late Christmas shopping with my wife and our six kids?'

Boss: 'Certainly not!'

Office manager: 'I knew you'd be understanding, sir. Thanks for getting me out of that terrible chore.'

88. Boss: 'Why are you late for work this morning?'

Office manager's clerk: 'I'm sorry, sir. Normally I dream of my favourite football team and wake up at 7 a.m. when the game is over – but this morning they had to play extra time . . .'

89. My boss is like a lamb. Whenever anyone asks for a pay rise or a day off he says: 'Baah!'

90. Employee: 'Sir, my wage packet this week was empty.'

Boss: 'I know. They don't make money in small enough denominations to pay you what you're worth.'

91. Office manager: 'Sir?'

Boss: 'Yes, what is it?'

Office manager: 'Sir, my wife said I should ask you for a rise.'

Boss: 'Hmm. I'll ask my wife tonight whether or not I should give you one.'

92. The rather absent-minded boss was sitting in his London office when the telephone rang. His secretary answered the 'phone and said: 'It's a long-distance from New York.'

'I know it is,' said the boss, continuing to read his newspaper. 'In fact, I think it's about three and a half thousand miles.'

BROKEN HOMES
93. I came from a broken home – the TV was broken, the furniture was broken, the windows were broken . . .

BUILDERS
94. Builder: 'I thought I recognised your daughter, sir. She was in the school that I was doing some work on. In the first

year, I believe.'

Harassed man: 'And which year was she in when you had finished the work?'

BUILDING SITE
95. Some workers were busy on a construction site next to a toy shop when suddenly they hit granite while digging a trench. They urgently needed some picks, but their base was about forty-five miles away and all the workmen were being paid a bonus for speedy completion of the work. What could they do?

Fortunately, the toy shop had a large display in one of its windows in which life-size teddy bears appeared to be working in a coal mine. Each teddy bear clutched a pick in its paws.

The construction workers approached the toy shop owner and he agreed to let them borrow the picks for the rest of that day; the workmen promising to use their own picks the following day.

After working for about three hours very successfully, the workmen stopped for a brief lunch.

Unfortunately, when they returned, they found that all the picks had been stolen – to which a passer-by commented: 'Didn't you know that today's the day the teddy bears have their picks nicked?'

BURGERS
96. What do you say to a burger? How now? Ground cow.

BUS DRIVER
97. The only reason he became a bus driver was because he wanted to tell people where to get off.

BUSINESS CARDS
98. I know a man who hands out blank business cards – he wants to remain anonymous.

C

CANNIBALS
99. I once met a cannibal who was constipated. I gave him some laxatives and he soon passed his cousin in the jungle.

CAR WASH
100. Cashier at car wash: 'That will be fifty pence, please. And seeing an Irishman like you this morning has really cheered me up.'

Irishman: 'How did you know I was Irish?'

Cashier at car wash: 'Well, we don't get many people riding motorcycles in here.'

CARPENTERS
101. It's easy for a carpenter to hammer in nails without hitting his fingers if he lets someone else hold the nail.

CARPET FITTING
102. Two men were fitting a wall-to-wall carpet in an elderly lady's house when they noticed a bump right in the middle of the carpet.

As they had finished fitting it, the workmen didn't really relish the thought of taking up the carpet again, especially as one of the workmen said: 'It must be that empty packet of cigarettes I was going to throw away.'

Thus, in order to get rid of the bump, the two workmen jumped up and down on it and it was soon flattened and the carpet now looked perfect.

Just then the lady came into the room and said: 'Excuse me, but I wondered if you had seen my budgie anywhere? It's hurt its wing and can't fly and so it just walks around on the floor.'

CARPETS

103. A friend of mine recently got a job selling carpets. I hear he's making a pile.

CARS

104. I once bought a car designed for five people: one had to drive while the other four pushed.

105. Janice: 'I think there's something wrong with the indicator lights on my car. Would you mind getting out of the car and calling out to me if they're O.K. or not?'

Janet: 'Certainly. Right. I'm ready. I'm looking at the indicator lights. Yes, they're working. No, they're not. Yes. No. Yes. No. Yes. No. Yes. No. Yes. No.'

106. One day Claude came home from work to find his wife painting one side of the car blue. She'd divided the car neatly in half and had already painted the other side bright yellow.

'What on earth are you doing?' asked Claude.

'Simple!' she replied. 'You know I've had so many accidents and I always get caught due to the statements of the witnesses in court. *Now*, if I have an accident, you watch them fight it out trying to decide what colour car caused the accident!'

107. After close inspection of the circumstances leading to over a million car accidents around the world, investigators have proved conclusively that the part of a car most likely to cause an accident is the nut behind the wheel.

108. Derek: 'This car you sold me is useless.'

Car dealer: 'What's wrong with it?'

Derek: 'Within a week of me buying the thing, one of the doors fell off it, all the lights failed, the exhaust dropped off, the brakes failed, and the steering wheel came loose in my hands. I thought you said the car had only had one careful driver?'

Car dealer: 'So I did. But the second owner wasn't quite so careful . . .'

CATS

109. A friend of mine used to own the most inquisitive cat in the whole of China. It was a Peking Tom.

110. John: 'I have one of the most intelligent cats in the world.'

Simon: 'What does it do?'

John: 'Watch me pretend to shoot it. Bang! You're dead!'

Simon: 'But the cat didn't do anything – he's still just licking his paws.'

John: 'That's what I mean about him being intelligent: he knew he wasn't dead.'

CEMETERIES

111. Little Julian had been carefully examining all the tombstones in the cemetery and reading all the various inscriptions when he suddenly asked his father: 'Daddy, where do they bury all the horrible people?'

CHICKENS

112. Farmer Smith made his chickens drink lots of whisky. He was hoping that they would lay Scotch eggs.

CHILDREN

113. Mavis: 'My children are terrible. They climb all over everywhere and never give me a moment's peace. How do you keep so calm?'

Ethel: 'It's all due to the wonders of a play pen. I sit inside it and the kids can't get me!'

114. Mrs. Smith: 'Have I told you about my children?'

Mrs. Witherspoon: 'No. And I'm genuinely grateful to you for not telling me.'

115. Amelia didn't know what to do with her seven-year-old son, Reginald. Every time a visitor came to the house or he saw someone he didn't know he would race towards them and bite them on the knee. Then he would cling to their legs and refuse to let go.

In desperation, Amelia took Reginald to a child psychologist and, on seeing the psychologist Reginald rushed towards him, bit his knee and then clung to the man's legs.

The child psychologist looked down at Reginald, then bent and whispered something in the boy's ear. Immediately, Reginald let go of the man's legs and ran back to his mother.

'He's cured!' cried Amelia. 'What did you say to him?'

The child psychologist smiled and said: 'I told him that if he didn't let go of my legs I'd smash his stupid face in.'

116. Samantha: 'Mummy, Friday always comes before Thursday.'

Mother: 'I'm sorry, dear, but you are wrong.'

Samantha: 'I'm not. Friday always comes before Thursday in the dictionary!'

117. The children were happily playing in the garden when little Freda asked John if he wanted his palm read. When he said he did, she took out a pot of red paint she had been hiding behind her back and tipped it all over his hand.

118. Mother: 'Who are you writing to?'

Four-year-old daughter: 'Myself.'

Mother: 'What does the letter say?'

Four-year-old daughter: 'Don't be silly! How do I know? I haven't sent it and received it yet.'

119. 'Mummy,' said five-year-old Brian, 'I've been very good and filled the salt cellar like you asked me to, but it's taken a very long time.'

'Why is that?'

'Because it was very difficult getting the salt in through that tiny hole in the top.'

120. Three-year-old Samantha had just been punished by her mother for telling lies. 'I never told lies when I was a little girl,' said Samantha's mother.

'Oh, mother,' sobbed little Samantha, 'so when did you start?'

121. Aunt: 'Now tell me, Juliet, what will you do when you are as big as your mother?'

Five-year-old Juliet: 'Go on a diet.'

122. Health visitor: 'Why do you keep having more children? You've already got nine – and now you're pregnant again!'

Woman: 'I know. But you wouldn't want the youngest child to keep getting spoiled, would you?'

123. 'Mummy, mummy! Look at me!' shouted six-year-old Derek while hanging twenty feet above the ground from a branch of a tree.

'Derek!' shouted his mother in reply. 'If you fall and break your legs don't come running to me!'

124. It has been said that children brighten a home. I suppose that's because they never turn any of the lights off.

125. 'Auntie,' said five-year-old Mandy, 'I don't think mummy knows how to bring up children properly. Can you speak to her?'

'Why? What has she done?' asked Mandy's aunt.

'I'm sure she doesn't know anything about raising children. She always sends me to bed when I don't feel sleepy and wakes me up when I'm still tired.'

126. Mother: 'Why are you crying?'

Sally: 'Because I fell over and hurt myself.'

Mother: 'When did you do that?'

Sally: 'About twenty minutes ago.'

Mother: 'But I've only just heard you crying – you haven't been crying for twenty minutes.'

Sally: 'I know. Earlier, I thought you'd gone out.'

127. Mother: 'Why did you put a newt in your sister's bed?'

Small son: 'Because I couldn't find a mouse.'

128. Father: 'What are you going to be when you've finished studying and passed all your exams?'

Son: 'Probably an old age pensioner.'

129. Small daughter: 'Mummy, how many more days is it before Christmas?'

Mother: 'Not many. Why do you ask?'

Small daughter: 'I just wondered if it's near enough for me to start being a good little girl.'

130. Mavis had told her daughter, three-year-old Fiona, to be on her best behaviour when she visited one of her aunts who was a stickler for good manners.

'Always say "please" and "thank you",' cautioned Mavis. 'And whatever you do, always be polite.'

Thus it was that at lunch when the aunt enquired of Fiona 'Can you manage with the meat? Or would you like me to cut it in small pieces for you?' Fiona replied: 'No, thank you. I can manage on my own, thank you. We sometimes have meat as tough as this at home.'

131. 'Bernard!' screamed Bernard's mother. 'Why did you fall in that mud wearing your new trousers?'

'Because,' replied Bernard, 'there wasn't time to take them off.'

132. Four-year-old Diana was looking expectantly at her rather plump aunt as she sat at the dinner table.

'Why are you looking at me like that?' asked the aunt.

'Well,' replied Diana, 'I'm waiting for you to get your nosebag out.'

'My nosebag?'

'Yes. I heard Daddy tell Mummy last night that you ate like a horse.'

133. Mother: 'Now, let's see how clever you are, Joan. If I have six sweets and someone gives me another two sweets, how many sweets do I have?'

Very young daughter: 'I don't know, mummy. At nursery school we do all our sums with fingers or apples.'

134. Very annoyed lady: 'I'll teach you to throw bricks at my greenhouse!'

Small boy: 'Thanks a lot, lady! When do the lessons start as I sure need them. My last five bricks missed.'

135. Terence: 'Mum, where do all the flies go in winter?'
Mother: 'Search me.'
Terence: 'No thanks. I believe you.'

136. Mother: 'Today you have a choice for dinner. You either eat it – or you leave it.'

137. Forgetful aunt: 'Hector, how old will you be next birthday?'
Hector: 'Six.'
Forgetful aunt: 'So on your last birthday how old were you?'
Hector: 'Four.'
Forgetful aunt: 'Four? How can that be if you will be six on your next birthday?'
Hector: 'Easy! I'm five today.'

138. My children have so many things in their rooms – TV, hi-fi system, books, games – that, when they are naughty, as a punishment I have to send them to *my* room.

139. Mrs. Gruntleburger was rather surprised at how well behaved her little niece appeared to be.

'You're very quiet,' she said. 'Why are you so well behaved and quiet?'

The little niece replied: 'Because mummy has promised me I can have a new teddy bear if I don't say anything about your enormous nose and funny ears.'

140. John: 'Mummy, Barry has just broken a pane of glass in the greenhouse.'

Mother: 'How did he do that?'

John: 'I threw my cricket bat at him and he ducked.'

141. Four-year-old Claire was a difficult child and didn't seem to want to eat anything other than chocolates and cake and biscuits.

'Come on,' urged her mother. 'Eat your dinner.'

'I don't want it,' said Claire.

'But there are millions of children in Africa who would be glad of a meal like that.'

'Then name one of them,' said Claire, triumphantly.

CHRISTENING

142. Rodney: 'Why are you so pleased your mother christened you "John"?'

John: 'Because that's what everyone calls me.'

CHURCH

143. Sarah is a regular church-goer – she goes every Christmas.

144. 'Next week,' said the vicar, 'my sermon will be entirely about truthfulness and I think it is especially important that on getting home from church today – or at least sometime during the week – that you read the twenty-ninth chapter of Leviticus.'

The following week the vicar started his sermon: 'Last week I said that my sermon this week would be about truthfulness and I asked you all to read the twenty-ninth chapter of Leviticus. Now, can all those who did this please raise their right hands.'

Almost the entire congregation raised their right hands.

'Just as I suspected!' said the vicar. 'And that is why my sermon today is about truthfulness. You could not possibly have read the twenty-ninth chapter of Leviticus. Leviticus only has twenty-seven chapters.'

145. Four-year-old James came home from a visit to the

church with his aunt and told his mother: 'I was very good and didn't give in to temptation. When they brought round a huge plate with money on it I said I didn't want it.'

146. Candida was eighty years old and one day she went to confession and said: 'Father, I have sinned. I have committed adultery with a seventeen year old gardener.'

'When was this?' asked the priest.

'Fifty years ago – but I just felt like recalling pleasant experiences this week.'

147. It was the little English girl's first visit to a church in the USA.

The clergyman was an extremely energetic preacher and during his sermon he stood in the pulpit and gestured wildly with his hands, shouted and wailed at his congregation, cajoled them, thumped the sides of the pulpit with his fists to emphasize certain points, and his facial expressions ranged from rage to kindness but all with extreme emotive passion.

As the clergyman stamped his feet and banged on his pulpit again, the little girl turned to her mother and whispered: 'I hope they keep him locked up in that little box – I wouldn't like to be near him if he gets out.'

CINEMA

148. I once went to a cinema and watched a mad, passionate scene that lasted for almost half an hour – then I had to stop looking at the back row and watch the film.

CIVIL SERVICE

149. When James graduated from Oxford he applied for a position in the Civil Service. At his selection interview he was asked: 'What can you do well?'

James thought for a moment and then replied: 'Nothing.'

'Good!' cried the selection panel in unison. 'You're just the sort of chap we want – and we won't even have to break you in!'

CLEANERS

150. Theodora had found it difficult to find a suitable cleaner for her luxury apartment and she was delighted when a domestic services agency sent her someone who, at long last, looked ideal.

Theodora gestured to some paintings hanging on one of the walls. 'These paintings have to be treated with the utmost care as they are old masters.'

'Really?' said the cleaner. 'I didn't realise you had been married so many times.'

CLERGYMEN

151. A rather stone-faced and cold, celibate clergyman died and, soon after, one of his best friends also passed away.

On arriving in the 'other place' the clergyman's friend was surprised to see the clergyman with two beautiful blonde ladies sitting on his knee, and a gorgeous black-haired lady was stroking his shoulders and all three were clearly trying to seduce him.

'I see you're being well treated,' said the friend. 'I didn't realise Heaven was going to be so good.'

'I'm not enjoying myself,' replied the clergyman with a sour look. 'And this isn't Heaven. We're all in Hell – and I'm these three ladies' punishment.'

152. 'My Catholic priest knows more than your Methodist minister,' said ten-year-old Nathan.

'Of course he does,' replied David. 'You have to tell him everything.'

153. Vicar: 'Now tell me, Freda, how many times a day do you say prayers?'

Four-year-old Freda: 'Once, sir. At night.'

Vicar: 'But don't you say any prayers at all during the day?'

Four-year-old Freda: 'No, sir. I'm only frightened at night.'

154. The vicar was giving a Christmas party for all the children who attended Sunday school when little Melissa put up her hand and said: 'Please reverend, can I whisper something to you?'

The vicar frowned and replied: 'I'm afraid not, Melissa. We should have no secrets from one another.'

Melissa paused for a moment and then said: 'Your flies have come undone.'

CLOCKS
155. Tom's grandfather collected clocks. By the time he died he had 2,378 different clocks and it's been taking Tom ages to wind up his grandfather's estate.

CLOTHES
156. My husband wears clothes that will never go out of style – they'll always look ridiculous.

157. Sally: 'I always know what to do to cheer myself up. Whenever I'm down in the dumps I get myself some new clothes.'

Samantha: 'So that explains it! I always wondered where you got such unusual clothes.'

COATS
158. Cyril's wife had moaned at him: 'I'm fed up with all these cheap coats you make me wear – all synthetic materials and horrible. Why can't you buy me a nice animal skin one instead?' So Cyril went and bought her a donkey jacket.

COCKTAIL PARTIES
159. It seems that at cocktail parties people believe they should only open their mouths when they have nothing to say.

160. A lady at a cocktail party lost her handbag and she persuaded her husband to bang on a glass and call for attention and say: 'Excuse me, everyone. But my wife seems to have mislaid her handbag. It contained some very personal items in it of great sentimental value – like two hundred pounds in ten pound notes. Whoever finds it I'll give twenty pounds as a reward.'

A voice from the back of the room called: 'I'll give fifty pounds.' This was quickly followed by another voice calling: 'And if anyone brings me the bag I'll give sixty-five pounds.'

COMPETITIONS

161. John: 'Why are you so sad? You've just won first prize with your raffle ticket and got yourself a brand new car.'

Brian: 'I know. But I bought two tickets and the other one didn't win anything so I wasted my money on it.'

COOKERY

162. Wife: 'I've made you three different sorts of cake today. Would you like to take your pick?'

Husband: 'No thanks, I'll use the hammer and chisel like always.'

163. Henry: 'My wife made me a very unusual dinner last night: toad-in-the-hole.'

Claude: 'What's so unusual about that?'

Henry: 'She used real toads.'

Claude: 'Thank goodness she didn't try to make spotted dick . . .'

164. Mr. Bloggs: 'Darling, I don't know what you put in this soup, but it tastes like dishwater.'

Mrs. Bloggs: 'How do you know?'

165. Mr. and Mrs. Smith were interviewing applicants for the job of cook for their country house.

One applicant seemed well suited for the job and he particularly appealed to Mrs. Smith because he was young and attractive.

'Tell me,' said Mr. Smith. 'What if my wife asked for a little extra after dinner? Would you be able to cope?'

The applicant smiled and said: 'Of course. I'm just as liberated as you two seem to be: I've had a vasectomy.'

166. When Mr. Smith came home from work his wife offered him a slice of cake, saying: 'I made this myself this morning. It's a new recipe I read in a woman's magazine. It tastes delicious, except for a slightly gritty taste.'

'Hmm,' said Mr. Smith, tasting the cake. 'It is just a bit gritty.'

'Well, I followed the recipe exactly, dear,' replied Mrs. Smith. 'But I did wonder about the two whole eggs the recipe said I should use. Maybe the shells weren't crushed up small enough.'

167. My aunt believes that the best way to make a Mexican chilli is to take him to Alaska.

168. 'Darling,' said Mrs. Bloggis to her husband. 'I do hope you'll like the sole. It looked a bit off so I fried it, but that didn't seem to do much to it. So I tried grilling it but it still looked funny. So now I've boiled it.'

169. Mrs. Smith: 'I've just read an interesting article. It said that most accidents that happen, happen in the kitchen.'

Mr. Smith: 'I know: you always expect me to eat them.'

170. My wife treats me like a pagan god. Every evening at dinner time she gives me a burnt offering.

171. Mother: 'The milk has boiled all over the stove. Just look at the mess! I thought I told you to watch when it boiled over.'

Ten-year-old son: 'I did, mum. It was 12.32.'

172. The owners of the small zoo were not doing very well and as they eventually used up all their savings they were forced to start eating some of the animals from their collection.

One day, when the husband came home carrying two baby

monkeys and one small dead bird his wife said: 'Oh no! Surely you don't expect me to cook finch and chimps again!'

COURT
173. Judge: 'How do you plead? Guilty or not guilty?'

Prisoner: 'How do I know, your honour? I haven't heard the evidence yet.'

174. When the prisoner appeared in court accused of stealing five skunks from the zoo the cry soon went up: 'Odour in court!'

COWBOYS
175. It was in the days of the old Wild West and the sheriff was hunting for a man who was dressed entirely in tissue paper. It seems he was wanted for rustling.

176. Hank: 'They call this here ranch the Lone Circle Triple Diamond Lazy Q Bar T Homestead.'

Clara: 'How many head of cattle do you have?'

Hank: 'Two. None of the rest survived the branding.'

COWS
177. Farmer: 'Stop it! Stop it! Why are you beating the feet of the cows like that and making them jump up and down?'

Brian: 'I'm trying to make a milk shake.'

CRAP GAME
178. My husband is so stupid he thinks a crap game is where people take bets on who can throw dried cow droppings the farthest.

CROCODILE
179. What do you call a crocodile at the North Pole? Lost.

CUFF LINKS
180. When Brian was given some cuff links for Christmas he went and had his wrists pierced.

D

DANCER

181. The go-go dancer was so bad everyone said she was more like a gone-gone dancer.

DATING

182. Jonathan was a successful businessman but he'd been so busy making money he'd never had time to find himself a proper girlfriend so one day he wrote off to a computer dating agency that promised him the perfect match.

He was delighted to receive the name of a girl who lived nearby and decided to 'phone her to arrange their first meeting.

'And I'll meet you in the lounge area of the Golden Fleece restaurant – but how will I recognise you?' he asked.

'Well, I'll be wearing my scarlet dress, with scarlet shoes and a round scarlet hat.'

'Oh!' cried Jonathan happily, 'I always knew you'd be one in vermilion!'

DEFINITIONS

183. Bacteria: the back entrance to a cafeteria.

184. Buoyant: male equivalent of gallant.

185. Catacomb: a comb for a cat.

186. Countdown: something they do in an eiderdown factory.

187. Dogma: the mother of puppies.

188. Filing cabinet: a useful container where things can be lost alphabetically.

189. Ghoulash: a cremated ghost.

190. Myth: unmarried female with a lisp.

191. Octopus: an eight-sided cat.

192. Polysyllables: the language of parrots.

193. Signature tune: song of a young swan (cygnet).

194. Ultimate: the last person to marry.

DESSERT
195. The favourite dessert of barristers and solicitors is sue-it pudding.

DIETS
196. When my husband went on a diet for two weeks all he lost was a fortnight.

DINNER PARTIES
197. The posh dinner party had been a great success until, over coffee, one of the guests decided to tell a long and intimately detailed blue joke.

The host of the dinner party was appalled: 'That was an outrageous joke! How dare you tell such a story before my wife!'

'I'm sorry,' replied the joke teller, 'I didn't realise your wife wanted to tell it herself!'

DISCOS
198. It was the first time forty-eight-year-old Avis Wigglesworth had been to a disco and she had only gone as a special favour to her daughter who had entered a dance contest at the disco and said she needed every supporter in the audience she could get.

As Avis looked around the room she muttered to the person standing next to her: 'This is an amazing place. And the people are even more incredible. Just look at that girl over there – dyed green hair, yellow jeans that fit like snake-skin, ten inch heels on her shoes . . .'

'That,' said the person next to Avis, 'is not a girl. That is my son.'

'Oh, I'm sorry,' said Avis, blushing with embarrassment. 'I didn't know you were his father.'

'I'm not,' was the reply, 'I'm his mother.'

DOCTOR

199. Doctor: 'Now, you see that bottle on the table over there?'

Male patient: 'Yes, doctor.'

Doctor: 'Well, I want you to give me a sample of urine in it.'

Male patient (amazed): 'You expect me to do it from here? But what if some falls on the carpet before reaching that far?'

200. The only reason doctors wear masks when they perform operations is so that no one can recognise them if anything goes wrong.

201. Doctor: 'Now, tell me, have you ever had any trouble with diarrhoea?'

Patient: 'Only once.'

Doctor: 'And when was that?'

Patient: 'When I was at school and was asked to spell it.'

202. Doctor: 'Nurse! Did you take this patient's temperature?'

Nurse: 'Why, doctor? Is it missing?'

203. Patient: 'Doctor! I don't know what's wrong with me but my body feels like jelly and my head has turned all yellow – as yellow as custard.'

Doctor: 'I think you must be a trifle ill.'

204. Patient: 'Doctor, I feel like a pack of cards.'

Doctor: 'Just sit down and I'll deal with you in a minute.'

205. Patient: 'Doctor! Can you give me anything to stop me from sleepwalking?'

Doctor: 'Here's a box of a special item that should solve

your problem. After you've got in bed for the night, sprinkle the contents of the box on the floor around your bed.'

Patient: 'What's in the box, doctor? Is it a powder that gives off a special odour?'

Doctor: 'No. Inside the box are drawing pins.'

206. Patient: 'Doctor, I think I have an inferiority complex.'

Doctor: 'Don't be silly. You really are inferior.'

207. Patient: 'Doctor, doctor! I keep talking to myself.'

Doctor: 'That's nothing to worry about. Lots of people mutter to themselves.'

Patient: 'But I'm a life assurance salesman and I keep selling myself policies I don't want.'

208. Doctor: 'I'm afraid your records haven't reached me yet from your previous doctor and my scales have just been broken by an enormously fat lady patient of mine. But can you tell me your average weight?'

Patient: 'I'm sorry, I don't know.'

Doctor: 'Do you know the most you have weighed?'

Patient: 'I think it was twelve stone nine pounds.'

Doctor: 'And what was the least you've weighed?'

Patient: 'I think that was about seven pounds three ounces.'

209. Doctor: 'Do you snore at night?'

Patient: 'Only when I'm asleep.'

210. Patient: 'I feel like a very old sock.'

Doctor: 'Well, I'll be darned!'

211. American doctor: 'I don't know how to put this, but if I recommended that you had an operation, would you be able to pay for it?'

American patient: 'If I couldn't pay for it, would you still recommend that I had the operation, or some other cure?'

212. The doctor looked at the man in front of him who was only about five feet tall, but who was also probably five feet wide: totally obese!

'Hmm,' said the doctor, producing two enormous pills which weighed about fifty pounds each.

'But I can't possibly swallow huge pills like that,' protested the obese man.

'Who said you had to swallow them?' asked the doctor. 'All you've got to do is pick them up and raise them over your head and keep putting them down and picking them up for an hour a day.'

213. A doctor and his wife were sitting in deck chairs on the beach when a beautiful young girl in a very brief bikini jogged towards them. As she came to the doctor she waved at him and said, in a huskily sexy voice: 'Hi, there!' before continuing on her way.

'Who was that?' demanded the doctor's wife.

'Oh, just someone I met professionally,' replied the doctor.

'Oh, yes!' snorted the wife. 'Whose profession? Yours or hers?'

214. Patient: 'Doctor, people keep ignoring me.'
Doctor: 'Next patient, please!'

215. The man staggered into the doctor's surgery. He had three knives protruding out of his back, his head was bleeding from a gunshot wound, and his legs had been badly beaten by a hockey stick.

The doctor's receptionist looked up at this pitiful sight and said: 'Do you have an appointment?'

216. Patient: 'Doctor, doctor! I'm a kleptomaniac.'
Doctor: 'Are you taking anything for it?'

217. Doctor: 'Have you ever had your eyes checked?'
Patient: 'No, doctor. They've always been brown.'

218. Patient: 'Doctor, I keep thinking I'm a pair of curtains.'
Doctor: 'Well, pull yourself together.'

219. Patient: 'Doctor, I keep thinking I'm a dwarf who likes backing race horses.'

Doctor: 'There! Didn't I say those pills would make you feel like you were a little better!'

220. Patient: 'Doctor, my wooden leg keeps giving me the most awful pain.'

Doctor: 'Don't be ridiculous! How can a wooden leg give you pain?'

Patient: 'My wife keeps hitting me on the head with it.'

221. Patient: 'I've got bananas growing out of my ears.'

Doctor: 'Good gracious! How did that happen?'

Patient: 'I beg your pardon?'

222. Patient: 'Doctor, doctor! I think I'm becoming invisible.'

Doctor: 'Who said that?'

223. Patient: 'Doctor, do you think that I will live until I'm a hundred?'

Doctor: 'Do you smoke or drink?'

Patient: 'No, doctor, never.'

Doctor: 'Do you drive fast cars, gamble, or play around with women?'

Patient: 'Certainly not!'

Doctor: 'Then what do you want to live until a hundred for?'

224. Patient: 'Doctor, doctor! You've got to help me. I've just swallowed half a tin of gold paint.'

Doctor: 'How do you feel?'

Patient: 'Gilty.'

225. Patient: 'Doctor, you've already said that the operation is very risky. What are my chances of survival?'

Doctor: 'Excellent! The odds against success are 99 to 1, but the surgeon who will be performing the operation on you is looking forward to it as you will be his hundredth patient and so you must be a success after all the others!'

226. Patient: 'Doctor, doctor! I keep thinking I'm a clock.'
  Doctor: 'That sounds rather alarming! But don't you worry – we'll soon find out what makes you tick.'

227. Patient: 'Doctor! I keep thinking I'm a chicken.'
  Doctor: 'How long have you thought that?'
  Patient: 'For about a year.'
  Doctor: 'Why didn't you come and see me earlier?'
  Patient: 'Because my wife said we needed the eggs.'

228. Patient: 'Doctor, doctor! What do I need for ingrowing toenails?'
  Doctor: 'Ingrowing toes.'

229. Patient: 'Doctor, I think I'm turning into a chihuahua.'
  Doctor: 'Why not sit down and tell me all about it?'
  Patient: 'I can't. Dogs aren't allowed on the furniture.'

230. A trade union leader went to his doctor for help in getting to sleep. The doctor was reluctant to put the union leader on sleeping pills until other remedies had been tried and so he asked the man to lie quite still in bed at night and count sheep.

The trade union leader did this, but by the time he'd counted the twenty-seventh sheep they'd all gone on strike for shorter hours and lower fences.

231. Patient: 'Doctor! My head feels all stuffed up, my sinuses are blocked, and my waterworks don't work properly.'

Doctor: 'It seems to me that you'd be better off visiting a plumber instead of me.'

232. A man walked into the doctor's surgery and said: 'Can you help me? I've suddenly got a funny feeling in my head – it's all hot and I can't see. I also walk with a limp as one leg seems shorter than the other.'

The doctor looked at him thoughtfully for a moment and then said: 'It might help if you took your left boot off your head and put it back on your foot.'

233. Patient: 'Doctor! I keep feeling I'm a bell.'

Doctor: 'Well, give me a ring when you're feeling a bit better.'

234. Doctor: 'I want you to take these two pills.'

Patient: 'What are they for?'

Doctor: 'The pink pill is to make you get some sleep – and you take the green pill if you don't wake up.'

235. Doctor: 'And what have you come to see me about?'

Patient: 'Well, as you know, I used to think I was schizophrenic – but now both of us are all right.'

236. Doctor: 'How do you feel today?'

Patient: 'With my hands – just like I usually do.'

237. 'Doctor! I think I've just taken a turn for the nurse.'

238. Mother: 'My son can't stop biting nails.'

Doctor: 'How old is your son?'

Mother: 'Fifteen.'

Doctor: 'That's not unusual. Even at his age some people still bite their nails when they're nervous . . .'

Mother (interrupting): 'But he bites long nails he's pulled out of the floorboards!'

239. Patient: 'Doctor, why did the receptionist rush out of the room screaming?'

Doctor: 'When she asked you to strip to the waist ready for my examination she meant you to strip from the neck down, not from the toes up!'

240. Nurse: 'Doctor, why are you trying to write that prescription with a thermometer?'

Absent-minded doctor: 'Drat! some silly bum must have my biro!'

241. The little purple creature from another planet came to Earth and starting curing everyone who was ill with its wonderful pills and potions.

This proved too much for all the doctors who were in danger of losing their livelihoods so they took the little purple creature to court and sued it for alienation of infections.

242. Patient: 'Doctor, my depression is getting worse and worse. I think I'll end up committing suicide.'

Doctor: 'In that case, can I have my fee first?'

243. Patient: 'Doctor! I feel as if I'm at death's door.'

Doctor: 'Don't worry. I'll soon pull you through.'

244. Doctor: 'Did you do as I directed and take your medicine after your bath?'

Patient: 'I tried to, doctor, but after drinking the bath I didn't really have room to drink the medicine as well.'

245. Mr. Jones was on the 'phone talking to the doctor's receptionist. 'It's my son,' he said. 'He's only three years old and he's swallowed a pencil sharpener.'

The receptionist said: 'Don't worry. I'll send the doctor straight around to see you. Have you done anything yet yourself?'

'Yes,' replied Mr. Jones. 'I've sharpened my pencils with a penknife instead.'

246. Patient: 'You gave me these pills last week, doctor, but I'm still ill as it's impossible to follow the instructions on the bottle.'

Doctor: 'Why is that?'

Patient: 'Well, it says "take one pill three times daily" so I took one pill and thought it would fall out of me somewhere so I could take it again twice more that day – but I'm still waiting for it to come out!'

247. Patient: 'Doctor, I'm worried about my declining powers.'

Doctor: 'You mean your sexual powers?'

Patient: 'Yes.'

Doctor: 'But at ninety-three that's only to be expected.'

Patient: 'But Bill Smith is five years older than me and he

says he still makes love to his wife every other night.'

Doctor: 'Surely you can *say* the same?'

248. Doctor: 'Why do you think you've become schizo-phrenic?'

Patient: 'It was the only way I could think of to prove that two could live as cheaply as one.'

249. Doctor's wife: 'Why are you looking so worried, dear?'

Doctor: 'I think I've at last cured that Smith fellow.'

Doctor's wife: 'So why are you so worried?'

Doctor: 'I've given him so many pills and potions I can't work out which one worked.'

DOGS

250. Two dogs were walking along the pavement. Suddenly, one dog stopped and said: 'My name is Bonzo. What's your name?'

The other dog scratched and thought for a bit, and then replied: 'Well, I think it's Get Down Boy.'

251. When my friend's dog was faced with four trees he didn't have a leg to stand on.

252. Henrietta: 'Whenever we go out we let our puppy stay at home to look after the children.'

Clara: 'Is that safe?'

Henrietta: 'Of course. It's a baby setter.'

DRESSES

253. I always dress to please my husband – I make each dress last at least ten years.

DRIVING INSTRUCTOR

254. Driving instructor: 'What would you do if you were coming down that very steep hill into town and your brakes failed?'

Lady learner: 'Hit something cheap?'

DRUNK

255. The drunk staggered along the street with a large bottle of brandy in each pocket when he suddenly tripped and fell heavily to the ground.

As he began to pull himself to his feet he noticed that part of him felt wet. He touched the wet patch with his fingers, then looked blearily at his fingers and sighed: 'Thanksh goodnesh! It'sh only blood.'

E

ELECTRICIANS

256. Mrs. Smith: 'Why have you come today? You were supposed to repair the doorbell yesterday.'

Electrician: 'I did come yesterday but after I rang three times and got no answer I thought you must be out.'

ELEPHANTS

257. Why has an elephant got Big Ears?

Because Noddy refuses to pay the ransom money.

258. Simon: 'How do you make an elephant fly?'

Clara: 'Use a very large zip.'

259. The only reason elephants never forget is because they have nothing to remember.

ELVES

260. One of the elves was getting rather fat so his wife sent him away to the Elf Farm.

ENEMIES

261. It was in the days of old when the man came riding into the noble's castle at great speed. As soon as his horse had entered the inner courtyard of the castle, the man leapt off his horse and ran to the noble's reception room.

'Sire! Sire! I and my men have done as you wished and raped and pillaged in the North.'

'Fool!' snapped the noble. 'I told you to rape and pillage in the West. I have no enemies in the North.'

'Sire!' replied the man, 'you do now.'

262. My uncle doesn't have any enemies – it's just that all his friends hate him.

ENTHUSIASM

263. Mark: 'I throw myself into everything I do.'
Sally: 'Go and dig a large hole.'

EXCUSES

264. Charles was on his way home from the office when his car broke down in a small, winding lane. As he began to walk towards the farmhouse in the distance where he hoped to be able to telephone for help, a bright yellow sports car screeched to a halt.

'Can I help?' asked a gorgeous young lady in the sports car.

Charles explained the situation and the young lady explained that she lived in a small village about five miles away. She would take him home, offer him dinner, and he could 'phone a garage from her house.

Charles readily accepted her offer – including the dinner invitation – and thus it was that he eventually got his car repaired and arrived back home in the early hours of the morning.

'Where do you think you've been?' screamed his wife. 'Out all hours, no thought about me . . .'

'The car broke down and I was helped out by a gorgeous young girl in a sports car and I ended up having dinner with her at her house and then . . .'

'Don't say any more!' shrieked his wife. 'I've had enough of your lies. You've been out with the lads again playing cards!'

F

FARMERS

265. 'This is outrageous!' shouted the middle-aged man to the farmer's wife. 'You charge us a small fortune for camping in your field with absolutely no facilities at all and then one of the bees from one of your hives goes and stings me.'

'Well,' replied the farmer's wife. 'If you can show me which bee it was that stung you I'll hit it with my husband's cricket bat.'

266. Farmer Smith has just invented a new device which enables him to count his cows in the field quickly. He calls his invention a cowculator.

FATHER CHRISTMAS

267. It is said that you can always recognise an Irish Father Christmas as he's the one with a sack full of Easter eggs.

FILMS

268. I know a man who keeps making films about ducks. He seems to be hooked on making duckumentaries.

FIREFLY

269. I've just buried a very unfortunate firefly. It met its death trying to make love to a cigarette end.

FISH

270. One little niece of mine thought that a kipper was a fish that slept a lot.

FLOWERS

271. 'Darling, I'm afraid the florist made a mistake over my anniversary order for you and they've given me these large Brazilian ferns instead of your favourite anemones.'

'That's all right, dear. They're beautiful! With fronds like these who needs anemones?'

FOOTBALL

272. A man and his wife went to the ticket office at Plymouth football ground and handed over a twenty pound note, and said: 'Two, please.'

'Thank you,' replied the man in the ticket office. 'Would you like the goalkeeper and the centre forward – or are there two other players you'd like to buy instead?'

273. Football player: 'I don't know what to say. I feel so ashamed for missing that goal, I could kick myself.'

Football Club Manager: 'Let me do it for you – you're sure to miss.'

FOUR-LETTER WORDS

274. My wife is against four-letter words – like dust, cook, wash . . .

G

GARDENING

275. My daughter has a foolproof method of telling whether or not a plant is a weed. She pulls up everything in the garden and then she knows that whatever comes up again must be a weed.

276. Amanda: 'Why are you putting that evil-smelling green powder all over your garden?'

Annabel: 'To keep the crocodiles off it.'

Amanda: 'But there aren't any crocodiles around here!'

Annabel: 'See how good the green powder is?'

277. He's such a lazy gardener the only thing he grows in his garden is old.

GIRLFRIENDS

278. Henry used to go out with a girl who was very class conscious. He didn't have any class and she was very conscious of it.

279. I once had a girlfriend who was so ugly the only people who ever asked her to go to bed were her parents.

280. John's latest girlfriend is called 'Doorknob' – because she's been handled by so many men.

281. There I was, sitting in my girlfriend's house, snuggling up to her on the sofa, when suddenly she got up and turned off all the lights. So I took the hint and went home.

282. My latest girlfriend is known as 'Body' – because whenever I take her to parties people always ask me: 'Wherever did you dig her up?'

283. John's new girlfriend thinks that oral contraception is when she talks her way out of it.

GOLDFISH

284. Little Sarah's Aunt Hetty had arrived for tea and Hetty was rather concerned at Sarah's staring.

'Why do you keep staring at me, and then glaring at the goldfish bowl?' asked Aunt Hetty.

'Well I'm watching you and the goldfish bowl because I don't want to miss it when you do what I heard mummy and daddy whispering about: when you drink like a fish.'

GOLF

285. My wife claims that her golf is improving because today she hit the ball in one.

286. Andrew came rushing into the clubhouse in a state of great agitation. 'I've just sliced the ball into a tree but it re-bounded and went into the road where it hit the rider of a motorbike who fell off his bike and then a lorry ran into him causing its load of onions to spill all over the road which has caused more cars to crash and there are bodies and smashed vehicles all over the place. What can I do?'

The Club President thought deeply for a moment and then suggested: 'Take it a bit easier on the backswing in future.'

287. After his last shot, Mr. Smith turned to his caddy and asked: 'What do you think of my game?'

The caddy thought for a moment and then replied: 'I think your game is quite good. But I still prefer golf myself.'

288. Howard and Horace were playing golf when, by the side of the tenth hole, Horace suddenly stopped playing and watched a hearse and funeral procession drive slowly along a nearby road. As he watched, he lowered his head and took off his cap.

'That was very noble of you,' said Howard.

'Not at all,' replied Horace. 'A husband should always show some respect when his wife dies.'

GRANDMOTHER

289. 'Granny, can you do an impersonation of a frog?' asked three-year-old Sarah.

'Why?' asked Granny.

'Because,' replied Sarah, 'I heard mummy and daddy talking and they said we'd get a small fortune when you croak.'

290. Millicent was growing very rapidly and her mother was very proud of this and so wrote and told Millicent's grandmother that Millicent had grown another foot since the last time she had seen her.

Almost by return of post, Millicent's grandmother sent her another sock.

HAIR
291. John: 'When I proposed to you and we got married your hair was blonde. Now it's dark brown.'

Sally: 'So? Dark brown is my natural hair colour.'

John: 'I know that, now. I was just wondering if I could sue you for bleach of promise . . .'

HANDWRITING
292. Claude's teacher said his handwriting was so bad the only profession he could follow on leaving school was to be a doctor.

HEALTH FOOD RESTAURANT
293. Notice in the window of a health food restaurant: 'Our salad dinners will take your breadth away.'

HEARING AID
294. Cuthbert: 'I've just bought this amazing miracle of modern science – a hearing aid as small as a pea.'

Rodney: 'Was it very expensive?'

Cuthbert: 'It's almost one o'clock.'

HOLIDAYS
295. 'Mummy, mummy! Where are you?' cried the little boy on the promenade at Bournemouth.

'You poor little boy,' said an elderly lady. 'Come with me and I'll get you an ice cream and then we'll go and look for your mummy and if we still can't find her I'll take you to the nice man who rents out the beach huts and he'll get the police to look for your mummy.'

'I know where your mummy is,' said a small girl. 'She's . . .'

'Shush!' whispered the little boy. 'I know where she is, too, but this way I've already had two free ice creams this morning from other people before we found my mother – don't be mean and stop me getting a third one!'

296. Local: 'Lady! I'd come out of that sea if I were you. There are lots of sharks about.'

Lady tourist: 'That's all right. They're only man-eating sharks.'

297. A holiday is something you have for two weeks that takes fifty weeks to pay for.

298. Two middle-aged men were sitting at a beach-side café sipping lager when one of the men said: 'Hey! Look at that fat frump in the green costume. The one jumping up and down in the sea and waving. Most hideous sight on the entire beach. Do you think all that jumping up and down and beckoning and leering towards me is some kind of propositioning?'

'I don't know,' said the other man. 'If you like, I'll go down there and ask her: she's my wife!'

299. The weather was terrible for the whole two weeks of my holiday. I didn't get brown from the sun, but from the rust caused by the rain.

300. Jacintha: 'How was your holiday in Switzerland? Did you like the scenery?'

Sarah: 'Not really. You couldn't see much as the mountains kept getting in the way.'

301. Four-year-old Lionel: 'Mummy, can you buy me a metal detector, please?'

Mother: 'Why do you want one?'

Lionel: 'I'm hoping to find Daddy's watch with it.'

Mother: 'I didn't know Daddy had lost his watch.'

Lionel: 'He hasn't. But I was hoping if I had a metal detector and it picked up where Daddy's watch was buried that would also show me where I've buried Daddy in the sand.'

302. One year my wife and I decided to stay at a hotel that was advertised as being 'only a stone's throw from the beach.' The advertisement was certainly correct: thrown stones had broken all the hotel windows.

303. Simon: 'I know of only one way that a girl can remain a good girl on holiday in Greece.'

Hazel: 'And what way is that?'

Simon: 'I was right! I thought you wouldn't know.'

304. The last time I went on holiday for a fortnight it only rained twice: the first time for seven days, and the second time for a week.

305. Five-year-old Lionel: 'Mummy, can I go in the sea?'

Mother: 'Not today, Lionel. Maybe tomorrow. The sea is far too rough and choppy now.'

Lionel: 'But Daddy is in the sea swimming.'

Mother: 'I know, dear. But he's got lots of life assurance cover.'

306. For the first time in twenty years, Mr. and Mrs. Jones decided to take their holidays apart from each other. Mrs. Jones went to visit relatives in the U.S.A. while Mr. Jones went to Thailand.

The weather in Thailand was fantastic and Mr. Jones had a wonderful time, especially after he met a sexy young Thai massage girl called Sunny.

Indeed, the girl and the location must have gone to his head as he sent a postcard to his wife on which he wrote: 'The weather is here. Wish you were Sunny.'

HOMESICK

307. Janice: 'I'm feeling rather homesick.'

George: 'But you *are* at home!'

Janice: 'I know. But I'm sick of it.'

HONEYMOONS

308. After our honeymoon I felt like a new man. My wife

said she felt like one, too.

HORSES

309. My horse likes to gamble. Every time we come to a fence or a gate he tosses me for it.

310. Claire: 'Mummy, is it true that horses have six legs?'

Mother: 'Whatever makes you think that?'

Claire: 'Well, I heard that a horse has forelegs at the front and two at the back.'

HOSPITALS

311. When Algernon swallowed a boomerang he returned home from hospital and was re-admitted ninety-eight times.

312. Visitor: 'Excuse me, but can you tell me which ward Vera Ogglebuggy is in.'

Receptionist: 'Ah, yes. Wasn't she the lady who was run down by a steamroller earlier this morning?'

Visitor: 'Yes.'

Receptionist: 'Well, she's in Wards 7, 8, 9, 10 and 11.'

313. Trainee nurse: 'Who is that man over there?'

Nurse: 'He's famous throughout the whole hospital for his unconscious humour.'

Trainee nurse: 'Unconscious humour?'

Nurse: 'Yes. He's an anaesthetist.'

314. Voice on the 'phone: 'Hello? Is that the maternity hospital?'

Receptionist: 'Yes.'

Voice on the 'phone: 'Can you please send an ambulance round, the wife is about to have a baby.'

Receptionist: 'Is this her first baby?'

Voice on the 'phone: 'No. This is her husband.'

HOTELS

315. The irate guest stormed down to the reception clerk at the small hotel in Aruba in the Netherlands Antilles.

'I'm fed up!' exclaimed the guest. 'I can't sleep for the noise of all the mice scampering about all over the room.'

'Mice?' queried the receptionist. 'Do you have a fifteen florin or a twenty-five florin a night room?'

'Twenty-five florin.'

'Well,' said the receptionist. 'With respect, sir, those can't be mice – they must be rats!'

316. I once stayed in a hotel where the walls of our room were so thin every time I asked my wife a question I got three different answers.

317. Robert: 'That's the last time I stay in such a posh hotel.'
   Alan: 'Why, what was wrong with it?'
   Robert: 'They even made me wear a jacket and tie when I was in the sauna.'

318. I once stayed at a hotel in Venice that was so damp there was a goldfish in the mousetrap!

319. Mr. Smith: 'Do you have a room for tonight?'
   Hotel receptionist: 'Do you have a reservation?'
   Mr. Smith: 'No. I'm not a Red Indian.'

320. I once stayed in a hotel where the owners were so mean they even stole towels from the guests.

321. Hugh once stayed in a hotel in Thailand where they catered for a guest's every whim.

   The first night he was in his hotel room when the manager knocked on the door and called out: 'Do you have a girl in your room?'

   When Hugh called back 'No!' the manager asked: 'Do you want one?'

322. I once stayed in a hotel that was so large, to call room service you had to dial long distance.

HUSBANDS

323. 'It was the bells that killed my husband,' sobbed the nineteen-year-old girl at the funeral of her ninety-eight-year-old husband.

'All week,' she continued, 'he would save up his strength so that we could make love on a Sunday morning. He liked to do it to the rhythm of the church bells. If that stupid ice cream van hadn't gone past chiming its stupid tune I'm sure he would still be here today.'

324. My husband is so stupid every time he scratches his head he gets splinters in his fingers.

325. Henrietta: 'Why is your husband asleep on top of the chandelier?'

Wilhelmina: 'Oh – that's because he's a light sleeper.'

326. My husband can trace his ancestors back to royalty – King Kong.

327. I wish my husband had been born in the Dark Ages – he looks awful in the light.

328. My husband has given me something to live for – revenge.

329. My husband still looks like he did fifty years ago: ugly.

330. My husband is so stupid even Irishmen tell jokes about him.

331. Sally: 'I think my husband must have a sixth sense.'
Sarah: 'Why?'
Sally: 'Because there's no sign of the other five.'

332. Sally: 'My husband gives me everything I want.'
Samantha: 'Maybe that's because you don't want enough?'

333. My husband has always been enormously fat. Even as a baby he was fat. He was born on the 21st, 22nd, 23rd, 24th and 25th of July.

334. The only time people look up to my husband is when he walks around on stilts.

335. My husband was a premature baby – he was born before his parents were married.

336. I used to wonder where my husband went every evening. Then I came home early one night from one of my regular bingo evenings – and there he was: at home!

337. My husband has even teeth – it's a pity all the odd ones are missing.

338. My husband drinks so much that whenever I find him asleep and snoring on the sofa I know that liquor mortis has set in.

339. Janet: 'My husband is no good.'
   Julia: 'But I thought you told me last week that he was a model husband?'
   Janet: 'He is a model husband – but not a working model.'

340. My husband is so fat he doesn't take a bath – he goes to stand in the car wash.

341. My husband is so unlucky even his plastic flowers die.

342. My husband is a man of rare gifts – he rarely gives me any.

343. If my husband genuinely loved me he would have married someone else.

I

IDENTITY PARADES
344. At one identity parade in Ireland fifteen people were made to stand in a line – and then a pickpocket was brought in and asked to point out which people he'd robbed.

IMPRESSIONS
345. Three-year-old Clara likes to do bird impressions – she eats worms.

INLAND REVENUE

346. The frantic-looking lady came rushing out of her house into the street and cried: 'Help! Help! My young son has swallowed a coin and is choking. I don't know what to do!'

The people in the street all looked the other way, except for one middle-aged gentleman who rushed into the lady's house, found her young son, turned him upside down and shook him until the coin fell out of his mouth.

'Oh, thank you!' cried the lady, in happiness. 'Are you a doctor?'

'No, madam,' replied the middle-aged man. 'I'm with the Inland Revenue.'

INSECTICIDE

347. A friend of mine has just invented a wonderful new insecticide. You spray it on all your plants and it promptly kills them so that the insects will then starve to death.

INSURANCE

348. I've just bought a retirement policy. If I keep paying the premiums for thirty-five years the insurance salesman can retire rich.

349. Insurance salesman: 'Surely your husband needs more life insurance? I mean, if your husband suddenly dropped dead, what would you do?'

Mrs. Smith: 'I'd probably get a pet dog instead.'

350. When Mr. Smith read the small print on his double indemnity policy he discovered that if he died he would be buried twice.

INTERNATIONAL SALES EXHIBITION

351. At an international sales exhibition, one British salesman turned to another and asked: 'How are you faring so far today?'

'Quite well,' replied the other salesman. 'I've picked up

lots of useful information, followed up a number of promising leads, renewed relationships with a number of potential customers and made a lot of valuable new contacts.'

'So have I,' responded the first salesman. 'I haven't sold anything yet, either.'

INTERVIEWS
352. 'Now,' said the interviewer, 'before we start the interview proper I'd like you to take an intelligence test.'

'An intelligence test?' queried the job applicant. 'The advertisement in the newspaper didn't mention intelligence – it stated you were looking for a research assistant for an M.P.'

INVESTMENTS
353. Brian: 'You must think I'm absolutely stupid, asking me to invest in such a crackpot scheme.'

Fred: 'So I can put you down for a few thousand, then . . .'

ITCH
354. Mother: 'Why are you scratching yourself?'

Three-year-old Anna: 'Because only I know where I itch.'

J

JACUZZI
355. The first time a friend of mine went into a jacuzzi he thought he'd had a sudden attack of wind.

JELLY
356. When I worked in a restaurant in San Francisco I was asked to devise the most original dessert possible. So, being a staunch Republican, I made a mould in the shape of Ronald Reagan and was just about to pour the liquid jelly into it

when I was suddenly surrounded by FBI agents. They said they didn't want me to set a President . . .

JOBS
357. Millicent: 'My husband's career is in ruins.'

Mary: 'Oh, I'm sorry to hear that.'

Millicent: 'There's nothing to be sorry about. He's an archaeologist.'

JOKES
358. My husband can only tell jokes after he's drunk a whole bottle of whisky. It seems he has a rye sense of humour.

JOURNALISTS
359. He's such a terrible journalist the only time he gets scoops is when he's being served ice-cream.

JUMBLE SALE
360. I once went to a jumble sale and bought a very old and very large bureau. While I was cleaning it I must have pressed a secret button and a large panel in the back of the bureau popped open and three people fell out shouting: 'Where am I? Where am I?' That's how I realised I must have bought a missing persons bureau.

KIDNAPPING
361. Did you hear about the doctor who tried to be a kidnapper? He failed because no one could read his ransom letters.

362. Sally: 'Did you hear about the kidnapping this afternoon?'

Simon: 'No – who was it?'

Sally: 'My kid sister. She was napping and mum woke her up!'

KNOCK, KNOCK

363. 'Knock, knock.'
  'Who's there?'
  'A pair of knockers.'

L

LAS VEGAS

364. The easiest way to return from Las Vegas with a small fortune is to go there with a very large fortune.

LAUGHTER

365. What goes 'ha ha, hee hee, blonk'?
  Someone laughing his head off.

LAWNS

366. Two little boys were looking out of the window when they saw a lorry drive past loaded with turf.

'That's what I shall do when I'm rich,' said one of the little boys. 'I'll send my grass away to be cut, too.'

LIFE GUARD

367. Beach inspector: 'Why have you applied for the job of beach guard? You're just wasting my time! You can't even swim!'

Job applicant: 'I know. But at seven feet two inches in height I can wade out quite a long way!'

LIFTS

368. Customer of large department store: 'Why do you look so depressed?'

Department store lift attendant: 'Because my job keeps bringing me down.'

369. John: 'I hear that you've just joined a company selling lifts. How's business?'

Fred: 'Oh, up and down.'

LLAMAS

370. Henry: 'Look, dear! Look at this lovely llama I bought from the zoo.'

Gladys: 'A llama! Where on earth are you going to keep it?'

Henry: 'In my bedroom.'

Gladys: 'But what about the smell?'

Henry: 'Oh, I'm sure it won't mind that.'

LOST

371. The lorry driver was in Eastleigh in Hampshire when he slowed down his lorry and then stopped. Winding down the window of his cab he called out to a middle-aged lady: 'Excuse me, missus, but can you tell me the way to Southampton?'

'I'm sorry, I don't know,' replied the lady.

'Well, do you know which direction Winchester is in?'

'No.'

'Huh!' muttered the lorry driver. 'They can't be far from here and yet you don't know which direction they're in. You don't appear to know much.'

'At least,' responded the lady, '*I* am not the one who is lost!'

372. The little girl had been taken to the supermarket by her mother but had somehow managed to get lost near the tinned food section.

'Excuse me,' asked the little girl of another customer. 'Have you seen a mother walking along pushing a shopping trolley without a girl like me?'

LOVE
373. Algernon: 'I'd like to buy the woman I love a little cottage in the country where we can always be together.'

Cuthbert: 'So why don't you?'

Algernon: 'My wife won't let me.'

MAGAZINES
374. 1st student: 'Why are you saving all those old magazines?'

2nd student: 'Because I qualify as a doctor in five years' time and I'll need something suitable for my waiting room.'

MAGICIAN
375. The magician's former assistant whom he used to use in his sawing a woman in half act is now living happily in London and Monte Carlo.

MAIL ORDER
376. Henrietta (talking on the 'phone): 'Can I speak to someone in the mail order department?'

Voice on 'phone: 'Speaking.'

Henrietta: 'Oh. I'd like to order one. About thirty to thirty-five, fairly tall, reasonably well-off, and who likes animals.'

MARRIAGE
377. A beautiful nineteen-year-old girl was once asked why she had married a fat, balding, sixty-three-year-old man who

just happened to be very wealthy and own a number of large period houses. 'It's simple,' she said. 'I married him because I love his beautiful manors.'

378. My husband and I have a perfect marriage based on a give-and-take relationship: he gives and I take.

379. Small boy: 'Mummy, is it true that people can have sixteen marriage partners?'

Mother: 'Whatever gave you that idea?'

Small boy: 'Well, I've just watched that TV play and two people were getting married and the clergyman said they could have sixteen partners: four better, four worse, four richer and four poorer.'

380. Sarah: 'Lots of people keep asking me to get married.'

Sally: 'Like who?'

Sarah: 'My sister so she can have her own bedroom, my parents, my grandmother, my godparents . . .'

381. They got married in church after a fierce argument – it was Holy Acrimony.

382. After the sexy seventeen-year-old had married the wealthy old man she said to him: 'I'm glad we're married. Now I can protect you from all the other gold-diggers.'

383. When a friend of mine got married recently his wife was so fat that it took three people to carry her over the threshold of their new house.

384. Henry: 'My girlfriend and I want to get married in church. But do you approve of sex before the marriage service?'

Clergyman: 'If it delays the service – no!'

385. I only got married to please two people – my girlfriend and my mother.

386. When a reporter asked the young Hollywood actress if she was taking her marriage seriously, she replied: 'It *is* only my first . . .'

387. Reporter: 'Why have you been married nine times?'

Hollywood actress: 'I guess it must be because I like wedding cake so much.'

MARRIAGE BREAK-UP
388. Jeremy: 'If you don't mind me asking, why did your marriage to Julia break up?'

Jeffrey: 'It was due to sickness.'

Jeremy: 'I didn't know you or Julia had been ill.'

Jeffrey: 'We hadn't. I just got sick of Julia.'

MARRIAGE GUIDANCE
389. Mr. Bloggs: 'You've got to help me. My wife is absolutely unbearable. She insists on keeping a pet pig in the bedroom and the smell is terrible.'

Marriage guidance counsellor: 'Why don't you open the bedroom window and let some of the smell out?'

Mr. Bloggs: 'What? And let all my geese and pigeons escape?'

MASSEUSE
390. A friend of mine got a job as a masseuse at a very exclusive health club in London because she wanted to rub shoulders with the rich and famous.

MEDALS
391. Angela: 'My Dad's got hundreds of medals.'

Alicia: 'He must have been very brave in the last War.'

Angela: 'No – he got them in his job: he's a pawnbroker.'

MEN
392. The main difference between men and boys is that men's toys cost more money.

MESSAGES
393. Boss: 'Did you take any messages while I was out?'

Young secretary: 'No. Are any of them missing?'

MILITARY FAMILY
394. Sally: 'Did you know that my family has a long military history?'

Samantha: 'No.'

Sally: 'Yes. One of my ancestors even fell at Waterloo.'

Samantha: 'Why – did someone push him off the platform?'

MILITARY HONOURS
395. General: 'Can you tell me what a soldier must be before he can be buried with full military honours?'

Private: 'Dead, sir.'

MIND
396. Michael: 'I've just changed my mind.'

Sally: 'That's good! I hope it's better than your old one.'

MIND-READERS
397. Two mind-readers met in the street and one said to the other: 'Good morning! You're fine. How am I?'

MIRRORS
398. Sally: 'Whenever I see a mirror I can never resist looking into it for at least a few minutes to admire my flawless complexion. Do you think that's vanity?'

Samantha: 'No. More like imagination.'

MISER
399. When Edward called on his friend, Arnold (who was something of a miser) he found Arnold carefully stripping the wallpaper.

'Are you re-decorating?' asked Edward.

'Of course not!' replied Arnold. 'I'm moving.'

MISSIONARY

400. Annette: 'Why do you keep diving down into the sea with signposts?'

Missionary: 'Because I'm trying to save a few more lost soles.'

MODERN ART

401. Ethel: 'This modern art is so difficult to understand.'

Henrietta: 'Why? It's simple: if you can walk around it then it must be a sculpture, and if they've hung it on the wall then it can only be a picture.'

MOON

402. The Americans quickly proved that the Moon was uninhabited as one of the first things they did when they landed was to dig a hole. Since no one came to stand around and watch they knew that no one lived there.

MOTHBALLS

403. The box of mothballs I bought last week aren't very good. The house is still full of moths. Every time I throw a mothball at them they fly out of the way and I've only managed to hit one.

MOTHER-IN-LAW

404. My mother-in-law has got pedestrian eyes – they look both ways before they cross.

MOTHS

405. Jeremy: 'Why do moths fly with their legs apart?'

Justin: 'I don't know. Why do moths fly with their legs apart?'

Jeremy: 'Have you ever seen the size of a moth ball?'

MOUSTACHE

406. The Hollywood actor had to look seedy for his latest role and the make-up man gave him a moustache that had been made from the hair from a dog's leg. It made him look seedy all right – but whenever he walked past a lamp post the moustache curled upwards.

N

NEW YEAR'S RESOLUTION

407. Tim: 'What's your New Year's Resolution?'
    Frank: 'To be much less conceited.'
    Tim: 'Will that be difficult to maintain for a year?'
    Frank: 'Not for someone as clever and intelligent as me.'

NEWS

408. There was a serious motorway accident last night when a police van carrying three convicted thieves on their way to prison was in collision with a truck carrying a large load of cement. The prisoners escaped and the police are now looking for three hardened criminals.

NIGHTCLUB

409. Customer: 'Can you give me something long, cold and half full of vodka?'
    Waiter: 'How about my wife?'

NOSES

410. Simon: 'You have a beautiful nose.'
    Sally: 'Yes – I picked it myself.'

OCTOPUS

411. A man brought his pet octopus into the pub and said that he'd trained it to play any musical instrument in the whole of Britain.

At first, the pub regulars jeered, but after they had witnessed the octopus play a flute, the violin and then a saxophone their scepticism turned into virtual amazement.

Even more difficult and complex instruments were called for – and the octopus could play them all: the harpischord, tuba, and bassoon.

Then someone produced some bagpipes and the octopus appeared delighted – and proceeded to jump on them but did not produce any music.

'Why aren't you making music?' asked the owner of the octopus.

'Make music?' queried the octopus. 'I thought I was supposed to make love with it.'

OLD AGE

412. One of the first signs of a man getting old is when his little black book consists entirely of 'phone numbers of doctors, dentists and hospitals.

OPERA

413. I knew my uncle was a true opera lover when I caught him outside the bathroom door where our beautiful au pair was having a bath. She was singing an excerpt from *Der Rosenkavalier* and my uncle didn't peer through the keyhole to look at her gorgeous naked body – but put his ear to it!

OPTICIAN

414. 'I knew you needed an optician,' said the optician to the young man.

'How did you know that?'

'Simple! You just walked in through the window.'

P

PANTOMIME

415. When the Smith family went to the theatre to see a pantomime they found that all the actors had died of some strange disease and so the show was put on by the ghosts of the actors instead. So it was really a phantomime.

PARTIES

416. Lady Bloggis: 'We're having a party at the weekend to celebrate my daughter's coming out.'

Mavis Grunter-Tottle: 'How long was she inside – and what did she do?'

417. Algernon was boring everyone at the party. 'Yes,' he said, 'I've hunted all over India and Africa.'

'Oh,' asked a little old lady, 'what did you lose?'

PEARS

418. Small boy: 'I've just eaten six pears.'

Mother: 'Why did you eat so many – anyone would think pears grow on trees.'

PEOPLE

419. Henry: 'Why are you looking so miserable?'
Brian: 'Because people keep saying I'm anti-social.'
Henry: 'So?'
Brian: 'I'm not anti-social – it's just that I hate people.'

PHOTOGRAPHERS

420. The bossy, unattractive woman said to the photographer: 'Make sure your photos do me justice.'

'Madam,' replied the photographer, 'you don't want justice – you want mercy.'

421. Herbert's wife was trying to take a photo of him so she shrieked: 'Herbert! You're not trying again. Get in focus!'

PIANISTS

422. When Cyril visited the house of his least favourite nephew he was forced to endure the latter's not very good piano playing.

After he had finished his performance the nephew asked: 'How was that?'

'You should be on TV,' replied Cyril.

'You mean I'm that good!' said the nephew, clearly delighted.

'No. But if you were on TV at least I could turn you off.'

423. I learnt to play the piano in ten easy lessons. It was the first ninety that were difficult.

PIANO TUNER

424. Piano tuner: 'Good morning, sir, I've come to tune your piano.'

Mr. Smith: 'But I didn't ask for a piano tuner.'

Piano tuner: 'I know, sir, but your neighbours did.'

PIGS

425. Where do wealthy pigs in America live? In styscrapers.

PLANETS

426. Two planets were talking to each other when one suddenly asked: 'Who was the star I saw you with last night?' To which the other planet replied: 'That was no star – that was my sun.'

PLASTIC SURGERY

427. A man walked into the offices of a plastic surgeon and handed over a cheque for two thousand pounds to the receptionist.

'I think there is some mistake,' said the receptionist. 'Your bill is only one thousand pounds.'

'I know,'replied the man, 'but the operation was tremendously successful. The surgeon took some of the skin from my behind – where no one will ever see that it's missing – and grafted it on to my cheek and totally got rid of the large scar I used to have there.'

'So the extra thousand is for a job well done,' said the receptionist.

'Not exactly. It's a token of appreciation for all the delight I get every time my mother-in-law kisses my backside – and doesn't know it!'

POKER

428. Simon: 'Claude! Stop cheating with the cards.'

Claude: 'How do you know I'm cheating?'

Simon: 'Because you're not playing the hand I dealt you.'

POLICE

429. The police had hired the local village hall to give a talk about crime and other problems in the neighbourhood. The police impressed on all the inhabitants of the village that their community policeman was always available to assist in the prevention of crime and nuisances like children cycling on the pavement.

Thus it was that at 1.00 am the community policeman received a 'phone call from an elderly man. 'I can't sleep for all the noise,' he complained.

'What's causing it? Do you want me to make an arrest for breach of the peace?' asked the policeman.

'I don't know. It's two cats mating on the wall outside my house. They're making a hideous racket with all their love calls and things.'

'Cats!' exclaimed the policeman. 'Why don't you walk up to the cats, give one of them a sharp prod and tell it that he is wanted on the 'phone?'

'Will that make them stop?'

'It certainly stopped me,' said the community policeman, bitterly.

430. Policeman: 'I'm sorry, sir, but you will have to accompany me to the station.'

Simon: 'But why?'

Policeman: 'Because it's a dark and gloomy night and I'm frightened to go there on my own.'

431. Policeman: 'So you admit to shooting your wife?'

Scotsman: 'Yes.'

Policeman: 'And you say it was because you discovered she had six lovers.'

Scotsman: 'Yes.'

Policeman: 'But if you loved your wife dearly, which you say you did, then why did you shoot her instead of the six lovers?'

Scotsman: 'I wanted to economise on bullets.'

432. The police car, its siren blaring, raced in front of a speeding car and then manoeuvred itself to force the speeding car to stop.

A heavily built policeman got out of the police car and walked over to the recalcitrant driver.

'Your name, please?' asked the policeman, taking out his notebook and pen.

'Certainly, officer,' replied the driver. 'It's Horatio Xerxes Laertes Idomeneus Aeneas Asclepius Iphicles Menoeceus Memnon Philoctetes Tyndareus Hylas.'

The policeman thought for a moment, then looked at his notebook, shook his head and said: 'I'll just give you a warning this time – don't go breaking the speed limit again.'

POLITICIANS

433. The best politicians are the honest ones – when they're bought they stay bought.

POTATOES

434. My great-uncle is always trying to invent new types of vegetables. Yesterday he told me he's succeeded in crossing a sponge with a potato and he's calling them spongatoes. They taste a bit squashy – but they're very good at mopping up the gravy.

PREGNANCY

435. Juliet was triumphant! After five years of trying she had discovered that she was pregnant. But what was the best way of breaking this news to her husband?

She was so keen to share the news with him that she 'phoned him in his office and said: 'Darling, what would you say if you soon heard the patter of tiny feet around the house?'

'That it was time to move to another house,' replied her husband. 'I can't stand being in the same place as a lot of mice.'

PRESENTS

436. My husband said he wanted a big surprise for Christmas so on Christmas morning I crept up behind him and shouted 'Boo!' in his ear.

437. Algernon loved his elderly grandmother dearly and decided that for Christmas he would buy her a parrot as it would be someone for her to talk to and keep her company.

Algernon went to a pet shop and insisted that the parrot had to have a large vocabulary and he ended up paying a thousand pounds for what the pet shop owner assured him was the most talkative parrot he'd ever seen.

Algernon arranged for the parrot to be delivered to his grandmother on Christmas Eve and on Christmas Day he 'phoned his grandmother and asked: 'How did you like the bird I sent you?'

'It was delicious!' she replied.

438. When I won a fortune on the football pools my husband said he wanted to see the world – so I bought him an atlas.

439. John: 'I don't know what to buy my girlfriend for Christmas.'

Mike: 'What about some lipstick?'

John: 'I can't buy her that – I don't know the exact size of her mouth.'

440. When Mr. Bloggis left the company after fifty years of loyal service his boss gave him a comb as a gift. His secretary had said it would be a good parting present.

441. She was a girl who had everything – so her boyfriend gave her penicillin as a present.

PRISONERS

442. Eleven criminals have just escaped from a prison in Ireland by using a helicopter. Police have set up road blocks.

443. 1st prisoner: 'Why are you so unhappy?'

2nd prisoner: 'I've been sentenced to three hundred years in prison.'

1st prisoner: 'Cheer up! It could have been life.'

PROBLEMS

444. John: 'I've got a terrible problem. I've got a flat in Mayfair, an apartment in Spain, a condominium in Acapulco and I've just bought a three thousand acre estate in Surrey and my third Rolls Royce.'

Simon: 'What's wrong with that? You appear to be doing very well.'

John: 'But I only earn fifty pounds a week . . .'

PROFESSIONS

445. A surgeon, a Field Marshal and a politician had had a very liquid lunch together and were now in a deep argument.

'A surgeon's job is the oldest profession in the world,' said the surgeon.

'What makes you say that? asked the Field Marshal.

'Well,' replied the surgeon. 'When woman was created she was made from one of Adam's ribs and surely only a surgeon could do something like that.'

'Nonsense!' snorted the Field Marshal. 'Even before Adam and Eve there was a world and it is said that order was created out of chaos. Who else could do that but a soldier of the highest rank?'

'Ah!' said the politician. 'But who do you think created the chaos to be sorted out?'

PROPOSALS

446. Michael: 'Do you like nuts?'

Mavis: 'Are you proposing to me?'

PUB

447. Algernon went into a pub and ordered seventeen pints of beer. When the barmaid gave them to him he placed them in a line and then hastily gulped down the first glass, and then the third, fifth, seventh, ninth, eleventh, thirteenth, fifteenth and seventeenth glasses and then wiped his mouth with his sleeve and got up to leave.

'Don't you want the other drinks?' asked the barmaid.

'No thanks,' replied Algernon. 'My doctor said I could only have the odd drink . . .'

PUBLIC TRANSPORT

448. All buses and trains will be stopping today – to let the passengers on and off.

PUTT, PUTT, PUTT, PUTT, PUTT

449. What goes 'putt, putt, putt, putt, putt'?

A very bad golfer.

Q

QUESTIONS

450. Clara: 'Have you heard about the silly twit who keeps saying "no" to questions?'

Mary: 'No.'

Clara: 'So it's you!'

R

RACING PIGEONS
451. I know a man whose hobby is racing pigeons. Sometimes he's even faster than the pigeons.

RAIN
452. Colin and Mark were enjoying a quiet country stroll when suddenly they heard a noise overhead. Looking up they saw a large aeroplane and, as they watched, the door to the cargo hold burst open and hundreds of small parts intended for a Japanese motor manufacturer fell out.

'Watch out!' cried Colin. 'It's raining Datsun cogs!'

453. Mrs. Jones shouted at her small son, who was outside in the rain: 'What are you doing out there in the rain?'

'Getting wet,' replied her small son.

454. 'I have learnt some of white man's magic,' said the African Chief on returning to his country after a brief stay in England.

'What?' asked his brother.

'First, you must make a smooth piece of ground and get grass to grow on it. Then you carefully tend the grass. After that you place some sticks in the grass and get some men to put on all-white clothes. Two of the men have to carry pieces of wood called "bats" and another man has to carry a red ball. After a bit of running about between the sticks by two of the men and some throwing of the red ball, it will rain.'

455. I was once on a train with my wife and sitting next to us was a large Russian who told us that his name was Rudolf and that he was in England to attend an international conference on meteorology.

'Is that sleet or rain out there?' asked my wife.

'It looks like rain to me,' I said.

'I agree,' said the Russian.

'Well, it still looks like sleet to me,' replied my wife, who likes to argue about minor matters like the weather.

'Darling,' I responded calmly. 'It is raining. Surely you know that Rudolf the Red knows rain, dear?'

RED INDIANS

456. One Red Indian stayed indoors all day drinking tea. His friends worried about him and when he had not been seen for more than a week, his friends called on him and found him drowned in his own tea pee.

RESTAURANTS

457. Waiter: 'What would madam like for dessert?'

Customer: 'An assortment of your real cream ice cream – say, two scoops of chocolate chip, one scoop of vanilla, three scoops of banana, two scoops of strawberry and please cover the lot with thick chocolate sauce.'

Waiter: 'Certainly, madam. And would you like a few cherries on the top?'

Customer: 'No thank you. I'm on a diet.'

458. Waiter: 'Sir, would you like the chef's Surprise Pie?'

Customer: 'What's in it?'

Waiter: 'Chicken, sir.'

Customer: 'So what's the surprise?'

Waiter: 'The chef forgot to take the feathers off it.'

459. I once worked as a chef in a restaurant that only served food to midgets. In fact, I was a short order cook.

460. Chef: 'Sir, the waiter tells me that you don't like my famous lamb stew – yet I put my whole heart into it.'

Customer: 'That's probably what's wrong with it – you should have put lamb in it instead.'

461. Customer: 'Waiter! Does this restaurant ever have any clean tablecloths?'

Waiter: 'I'm sorry, sir, but I've only been here for six months.'

462. Customer: 'What are the prawns like today?'
Waiter: 'Like small pink fish.'

463. Customer: 'Waiter! This boiled egg is bad.'
Waiter (looking at the egg): 'So it is. Shall I pick it up and give it a good smack and tell it not to be bad again?'

464. Customer: 'Waiter! Will my pancakes be long?'
Waiter: 'No, madam. They will be round.'

465. Customer: 'Do you have any wild duck?'
Waiter: 'No, sir. But we can annoy a tame duck and make it wild.'

466. I was once in a small French restaurant when I saw a pretty young girl at the next table coughing and choking.

I quickly went to her aid and patted her back and she soon choked up a fish bone so I said: 'What's a plaice like this doing in a girl like you?'

467. Waiter: 'Would you like your coffee white or black, madam?'
Customer: 'Do you have any other colours?'

468. Customer: 'Waiter! There's a worm on my plate.'
Waiter: 'That's not a worm, sir. That's your sausage.'

469. Customer: 'Waiter! How much longer do you expect me to have to wait for my poached salmon?'
Waiter: 'I'm sorry, sir, but we are trying to hurry it up for you.'
Customer: 'Then can you assure me that you're using the right bait?'

470. Customer: 'Waiter! This meat tastes rather funny.'
Waiter: 'So why aren't you laughing, sir?'

471. Customer: 'Waiter! The kitchens in this restaurant must be absolutely spotless and germ free. You've obviously got a chef who must have something of a fetish about cleanliness.'
Waiter: 'Thank you for the compliment, sir. I'm sure the chef will be pleased.'

Customer: 'It wasn't meant to be a compliment. But you've confirmed my suspicions as to why the food tastes like disinfectant.'

472. Customer: 'Waiter! Your thumb is in my chicken soup.'

Waiter: 'That's all right, sir. The soup isn't very hot.'

473. Customer: 'Waiter!'

Waiter (walking slowly towards the customer, after having been engaged in a long conversation with three other waiters): 'Yes, sir?'

Customer: 'Are you the waiter who took my order?'

Waiter (consulting his notebook): 'Yes, sir.'

Customer: 'How are your new grandchildren?'

474. The old man had never been in an expensive restaurant and it was one of the things he longed to do before he died so he carefully saved a little of his pension money each week and eventually he had enough to dine out in style.

Unfortunately, he had a rude shock when he tied his table napkin around his neck and the head waiter in the restaurant said to him: 'Would sir like a shave or a haircut?'

475. Customer: 'Waiter! Get me the chef!'

Waiter: 'Certainly, sir.'

Chef: 'You summoned me, sir?'

Customer: 'I most certainly did! This steak and kidney pie is as hard as old rocks. It's absolutely terrible!'

Chef: 'But my steak and kidney pies are delicious. I've had lots of experience making them. Indeed, I've been making them since before you were born.'

Customer: 'So why did you have to wait until now to serve them?'

476. Mr. Smith was in a new restaurant that seemed to be staffed entirely by trainee waiters.

'What would you like for dessert?' asked one of the trainees.

'The cheese board, please' replied Mr. Smith. So the

trainee waiter scraped the cheese off it and gave him the board.

477. Customer: 'Waiter, there's nothing worse than finding a caterpillar in my salad.'

Waiter: 'Yes there is, sir. You could have found half a caterpillar.'

ROBBERY

478. Robber, brandishing a gun: 'Your money or your life.'

Mr. Smith: 'You'd better take my life. I'm saving my money for my old age.'

479. One robber was recently arrested for stealing a painting from an artist's studio. The painting was still wet and he was caught red-handed.

ROMANCE

480. Michael: 'I'm not feeling myself tonight.'

Mavis: 'That's good – now you can feel me for a change.'

481. The handsome young student sidled up to the young girl and asked: 'Are you going to have dinner anywhere tonight?'

The girl was flattered by his attentions, blushed, and replied: 'No – not that I know of.'

To which the handsome young student replied: 'What a pity – you'll be very hungry by tomorrow morning.'

482. Clarissa: 'Do you remember our holiday together last year?'

Jane: 'Yes, of course! How could I ever forget Greece?'
Clarissa: 'Do you remember, then, that boyfriend I had?'
Jane: 'Which one?'
Clarissa: 'The one I said life wasn't worth living without.'
Jane: 'Well?'
Clarissa: 'I've forgotten his name.'

483. Sally: 'Why are you holding your mouth like that?'

Jane: 'I've just had a mad passionate, burning kiss from my boyfriend.'

Sally: 'So what's wrong with that?'

Jane: 'He forgot to take the cigar out of his mouth first.'

484. Ethel: 'But Mr. Jones can't possibly be in hospital. Only last night I saw him in a restaurant looking perfectly fit and healthy with a blonde woman.'

Sally: 'So did his wife.'

485. Hector: 'If I asked you for a kiss, what would you say?'

Gloria: 'Nothing! It's impossible for me to talk and laugh at the same time.'

486. Amanda: 'I had to give up Cyril.'

Amy: 'Why, what was wrong with him? He looked ravishingly handsome, was reasonably well off, and you seemed to like him a lot.'

Amanda: 'He had a number of bad habits.'

Amy: 'But we all have those.'

Amanda: 'One of them was that he always stirred his tea or coffee – even in restaurants – with his left hand.'

Amy: 'What's bad about that?'

Amanda: 'Everyone else uses a spoon.'

487. It's easy to tell the difference between American, Chinese and Welsh girls.

American girls say: 'Gee, that was fantastic!'

Chinese girls say: 'That was wonderful. Now let's go and have a meal.'

Welsh girls say: 'Luv, the ceiling needs re-painting: do you think we can get the council to do it?'

488. Rodney: 'Is it true you're a home-loving girl?'

Sarah: 'Oh, no! I can make love anywhere.'

489. Samantha: 'Why are you moaning? You've just been given a huge diamond ring. Anyone else would be ecstatic.'

Sally: 'But the ring comes with the terrible curse of the Hyde-Whippenbrakes.'

Samantha: 'Oh – and what's the curse?'

Sally: 'With the ring comes Clyde Hyde-Whippenbrake.'

490. Clare: 'Darling, sometimes I think you only said you wanted to marry me because my aunt has left me a few hundred thousand pounds in her will.'

Charles: 'Don't be silly, sweetheart. I'd still want to marry you – even if someone else had left you the small fortune.'

491. Sally: 'I've had lots of men at my feet.'

Samantha: 'Shoe shop assistants and chiropodists?'

492. Sally: 'Wasn't that an amazing party last night? Pity I drank so much, I can't remember much of what happened, except I seemed to have had a wonderful time. Were you the man who made love to me under the table?'

Edward: 'About what time would that have been?'

493. Gwendoline's father, a doctor, did not approve of Terence, her latest boyfriend and had told Gwendoline what he thought of him and had also given her various other bits of advice.

Thus, when Gwendoline returned home after an evening out with Terence, her father asked her: 'Did you tell that dreadful Terence creature my opinion of him?'

Gwendoline, still thinking of earlier that evening, smiled and said: 'Yes.'

'Well,' demanded the doctor, 'what did he say?'

'You won't like it?'

'Come on!' said the doctor. 'Tell me.'

'He said he's not surprised so many of your patients ask for second opinions.'

494. Simon: 'Please, sir, I'd like to marry your daughter, Sally.'

Sally's father: 'Do you think you'll be able to make her happy?'

Simon: 'I *know* I can make her happy. You should have seen her last night in our hotel room . . .'

495. Errol: 'Darling, you mean absolutely everything to me! You're beautiful, talented, witty . . .'

Fiona: 'Thank you, darling.'

Errol: 'I know I'm not as handsome as Edwin, nor do I have a father as wealthy as his. And Edwin has his own luxury penthouse compared to my humble basement. But I really do love you and I so hope that you love me. Do you?'

Fiona: 'Of course I do! But who is this Edwin fellow? And what's his 'phone number?'

496. Hilary, the new groom, was in the middle of mucking out the stables when the boss's son walked in and exclaimed: 'You're pretty dirty, Hilary.'

Hilary smiled impishly and said: 'I'm even prettier when I'm clean.'

497. Percy: 'Something that happened to me in my childhood may have scarred me for life. It's something you should know about before we get engaged.'

Charlotte: 'What is it? What happened?'

Percy: 'When I was about five years old I was faced with a traumatic situation. There were elephants charging in front of me. A wild lion was leaping up and down behind me. And on one side of me was a horrible black panther.'

Charlotte: 'What did you do?'

Percy: 'I had no alternative but to wait until the roundabout stopped and I could get off.'

498. Hilary: 'You're the first man I've ever said "yes" to. In fact, I've said "no" to lots and lots of men.'

Herbert: 'What were they selling?'

499. The beautiful blonde snuggled up to the rich old man and sighed in his ear: 'Darling, I'd love to run my fingers through your hair – can you put your wig back on?'

500. George: 'Sir, I don't quite know how to ask this?'

Mr. Smith: 'Ask what?'

George: 'Well, I'd like your daughter for my wife.'

Mr. Smith: 'Don't be ridiculous! I know we live in liberated times, but I don't think I'd like my daughter to go off with your wife.'

501. Dorothy: 'I really hate that man! Norman has really got some nerve!'

Sally: 'Isn't Norman that doctor you were engaged to and then threw him over for George?'

Dorothy: 'Yes. But Norman couldn't take it in a civilised way. He's just sent me a letter asking for the return of the engagement ring and enclosing a bill for three hundred and six visits.'

502. Eighteen-year-old son: 'Dad?'

Father: 'Yes, son?'

Eighteen-year-old son: 'Did you ever make love when you were my age?'

Father: 'Yes, son. And let it be a horrible warning to you.'

Eighteen-year-old son: 'Why, what happened?'

Father: 'I ended up marrying your mother.'

503. Julia, snuggling up to Derek on the sofa: 'Dearest, you're a man in a million.'

'What!' shrieked Derek, pushing Julia away from him. 'There have been *that* many others!'

504. Claudia likes to bring out the animal in her wealthy new boyfriend – like mink, musquash . . .

505. Simon and Sarah were snuggled up on the sofa when Simon said: 'You know, I've been thinking. For the past few years I've been content just living on my own. But now I feel the need for a faithful companion. Someone who will always be there when I come home. Someone who will look at me with devotion in their eyes. Someone who . . .'

Sarah interrupted him: 'That's a great idea! Shall we go together to the pet shop and I'll help you choose the puppy?'

506. David: 'Last night I invited my girlfriend up to my flat for a surprise meal.'

Derek: 'Isn't she that gorgeous Chinese girl?'

David: 'Yes. So I thought I'd demonstrate my culinary arts and cook her something Chinese – but when I asked how she'd like her rice, boiled or fried, she replied "Thrown."'

507. Rodney: 'Who was that blonde I saw you with last night?'

John: 'That was the dark-haired girl you saw me with on Monday.'

508. Simon had been separated from his girlfriend for a week since he went to live and work in a neighbouring village. There was no bus service between the two villages, and – not having a car – the only way they could meet was to walk the three miles between their villages.

Thus, Simon wrote to his girlfriend:

'My dearest, darling Sally,

My heart pounds whenever I think of you. I love you more than mere words can tell. I would plunge to the depths of the deepest ocean, climb the highest mountain, cross the most desolate desert, take a rocket to the moon, or brave the coldest wastes of the Arctic Circle just for one glimpse of your adorable smile. I love you with all my heart, Simon.

P.S. I'll come over and see you Sunday – if it's not raining.'

509. Annette: 'Why are you marrying that hideously ugly old man? I know he's rich, but he's at least sixty years older than you.'

Angela: 'It's because he's got a very strong will – made out to me.'

510. A married man fell in love with a mermaid and everything went well with their affair until his wife began to smell something fishy . . .

511. Claude: 'I can't understand it! Wasn't it Julia who helped you give up drugs?'

John: 'Yes.'

Claude: 'And got you off the drink, too? And changed your diet for a much healthier one?'

John: 'Yes.'

Claude: 'So why have you ditched Julia and just got engaged to Clarissa?'

John: 'Because after all those changes for the better Julia

brought about in me I realised I could also do better than
her.'

512. Roderick was snuggling up to his girlfriend, Claudia,
when she suddenly said: 'Woof! Woof!'

'What did you say that for?' asked Roderick.

'Well,' replied Claudia, 'my mother told me that you'd
love me even more if I spoke in a husky voice. Isn't "woof,
woof" what huskies say?'

RUBBISH COLLECTORS

513. When John left school he went to the parks department
and asked if he could be trained to be a rubbish collector.

'But you don't need training for that,' said the parks
superintendent. 'You just pick it up as you go along.'

SALESMEN

514. John was at a cocktail party where he was boasting
about his latest sales success. 'And do you know how much I
sold?' he asked his bored victim.

'Probably about half,' replied the bored fellow.

'Half? What do you mean by half?' asked John.

'Half of what you will tell me you sold.'

515. The little old lady was busy dusting with her feather
duster in her little old cottage deep in the countryside when
there was a knock on the door.

'Good morning, madam,' said a sauve young man when
she opened the door, and he pushed his way into the house
saying: 'What a lovely house but I'm sure you'll be interested
in what I can offer you.'

'But . . .' started the old woman, before being interrupted
by the young man who had by now pulled a large bag of soot,

dust and other small items of rubbish from his pocket and was sprinkling them all over the carpet.

'Don't worry', said the young man, 'what I have in my car outside will soon remove all this rubbish, dust and soot and I'll even demonstrate by cleaning your other rooms, too. So effective is my new machine that it will even suck out ground-in dust and dirt like this' and he used his heel to drive into the pile of the carpet some of the soot.

'But . . .' tried the old lady, again, but to no avail as the young man had rapidly gone out of the front door and soon reappeared with a vacuum cleaner.

'Now, where can I plug this in?' he asked.

'Probably the next village, about ten miles away,' replied the old lady. 'The electricity supply hasn't reached here yet!'

SCHOOL

516. Teacher: 'Can anyone tell me what family the crocodile belongs to?'

Samantha: 'I'm sorry, miss, but nobody we know owns one.'

517. Teacher: 'What cake do you dislike the most?'

Young pupil: 'A cake of soap.'

518. Teacher: 'You've put your shoes on the wrong feet.'

Small boy: 'But these are the only feet I've got.'

519. Teacher: 'If I were to ask you to add 9,731 to 232 and then halve it, what do you think you would get?'

Simon: 'The wrong answer, sir.'

520. Teacher: 'Mavis, can you tell me which month is the shortest?'

Mavis: 'It's May, miss.'

Teacher: 'No, it isn't. The shortest month is February.'

Mavis: 'But, miss, February has eight letters in it while May only has three!'

521. Teacher: 'Lionel, can you tell me a word with four letters, that ends in 'k' and is another word for intercourse?'

Lionel: 'Really, sir! How could you ask such a question? You just want to get me expelled by saying a swear word!'

Teacher: 'Swear word? What swear word? The word I was looking for is "talk"!'

522. Teacher: 'Where are you from?'
New pupil: 'Devon, miss.'
Teacher: 'Which part?'
New pupil: 'All of me, miss.'

523. Teacher: 'Sally, can you name an animal that lives in Australia?'
Sally: 'A kangaroo, miss.'
Teacher: 'That's good. Can you tell me the name of another animal that lives in Australia?'
Sally: 'Another kangaroo, miss.'

524. Teacher: 'Now tell me, Millicent, where were English monarchs usually crowned?'
Millicent: 'On their heads, miss.'

525. Teacher: 'Can anyone tell me what Picasso and Braque have in common?'
Simon: 'They are both dead, sir.'

526. Teacher: 'Why can't you answer any of the questions?'
Pupil: 'So that I have a reason for coming to school. If I could answer them all what would be the point of being in your class?'

527. Headmaster: 'Why are you late for school?'
Pupil: 'I'm sorry, sir. But on the way I tripped and sprained my ankle.'
Headmaster: 'That's a lame excuse.'

528. Teacher: 'Now, Cressida, can you tell me what a cannibal is?'
Cressida: 'No, miss.'
Teacher: 'Well, if you ate your mother and father, what would you be?'
Cressida: 'An orphan, miss.'

529. Teacher: 'Freda! Dicephalous. Spell it.'

Freda: 'I.T., miss.'

530. Teacher: 'Everything you do is wrong. How can you expect to get a job when you leave school if everything you do is inaccurate?'

Pupil: 'Well, sir! I'm going to be a TV weatherman.'

531. 'Get up,' shouted Albert's mother. 'You'll be late for school.'

'But I don't want to go,' protested Albert. 'All the kids are horrible, the teachers are terrible, and it's all extremely boring. I want to stay home.'

'But,' replied Albert's mother, 'you're forty-three and the headmaster of the school.'

532. Teacher: 'Tell me, Amber, is the world flat or is it round?'

Amber: 'Neither, miss. My Mum keeps telling me it's crooked.'

533. Small boy: 'Please, miss, would you be angry and tell me off for something I didn't do?'

Teacher: 'No, of course not.'

Small boy: 'Oh, good! Then I can tell you I haven't done my homework.'

534. Angus was the teacher's pet. She kept him in a small cage near her desk.

535. English teacher: 'I'm sure if John Milton were with us today we'd still regard him as an exceptional man.'

Pupil: 'Yes, sir. Especially as he'd be well over three hundred and fifty years old.'

536. Teacher: 'Sarah, if it takes ten men two days to dig up a large garden, how long would it take five men to dig up the same garden?'

Sarah: 'No time at all, miss. The first ten men have already dug it up.'

537. Samantha: 'Please miss, Millicent has made a puddle on the floor.'

Teacher: 'Millicent! Why did you do that? Why didn't you put your hand up?'

Millicent: 'I did, miss. But it still trickled through my fingers.'

SCHOOL REUNIONS

538. It was ten years since William and Derek had left school and in those ten years they had not met.

Then, at the school reunion dinner, they sat next to each other.

'How has life treated you since leaving school?' asked Derek.

'Oh, I've had my ups and downs. But now I'm doing quite well as an estate agent. We've got offices in fifteen towns and villages in the area and hope to open a London branch next year.'

'That sounds good,' replied Derek.

'And how have you done since leaving school?' asked William.

'Not so good,' said Derek. 'You know when I was at school I fancied Fiona? Well, I married her soon after school – but within three months of marriage she left me for another man. Then my second wife ran off with her girlfriend. The new house I bought by the sea was a bit too near it – within a year after buying it the cliff it was on fell into the sea, taking the house and all my possessions with it. And you probably saw that I walk with a limp. That's the result of falling out of my canoe and being crushed against a weir. And today didn't start too well, either. My dog was run over and killed by a bus and my motorcycle was set on fire by vandals.'

'But, if you don't mind me asking,' said William 'What do you do for a living?'

'Oh!' replied Derek, 'I sell good luck charms.'

539. It was the class reunion and Derek went up to a man and said: 'I almost didn't recognise you. The last time I saw you I thought you looked quite ill: you were very pale and thin and your hair seemed to be receding. Now you look healthy, fit and have grown a moustache. Are you on a new diet or something Jeremy?'

'I'm not Jeremy.'

'Oh!' said Derek. 'Then you've changed your name to go with your new image?'

SEA
540. Why did the sea roar?

Because it discovered crabs in its bed.

SECRETARIES
541. Boss: 'Please file these letters immediately.'

New secretary: 'But filing them will take ages. Couldn't I just trim them with a small pair of scissors instead?'

542. 1st secretary: 'Do you like a boss who flirts with you, or the other sort?'

2nd secretary: 'Is there another sort?'

543. New secretary: 'You seem to know your way around very well. How long have you worked here?'

Secretary: 'Ever since the boss told me he'd sack me if I didn't.'

544. The secretary heard footsteps and hastily put down the 'phone as her boss came into her office.

'How many times must I tell you?' thundered her boss. 'You must *not* use the office 'phones for personal calls.'

'But I wasn't,' protested the secretary. 'It was a business call.'

'Then,' responded her boss, 'you might like to tell me which person it is that this company does business with who is called "darling sweetheart"!'

545. Boss: 'You've had days off already this month for your father-in-law's funeral, your son's christening, your daughter's illness, and your brother-in-law's wedding – why on earth do you want another day off work tomorrow?'

Secretary: 'I'm getting married.'

546. Charles: 'I hear your new secretary is fantastic to look at – but rather dim. Is that right?'

Claude: 'Well, she did spend all afternoon trying to 'phone a VAT number.'

547. The young girl applied to be an executive secretary and all went well at her job interview until she asked: 'And how much will I be paid?'

'You will be paid what you are worth,' said the personnel manager with a smile.

'Huh!' replied the girl, getting up and walking towards the door. 'I couldn't possibly work for as little as that!'

548. Office manager: 'Clara, you've been seen kissing a number of the male clerks in the stationery cupboard; have been observed cuddling the messenger boy; and today I find you canoodling with a trainee accountant. What sort of a reference can I possibly give you after that sort of behaviour?'

Trainee secretary: 'Perhaps you could say that while I was training I tried my best to please as many people as possible in the office.'

549. Mr. Smith's wife decided to make an unexpected visit to her husband's office in order to take a look at his new secretary.

'You liar!' hissed Mrs. Smith to her husband. 'You told me that your new secretary was very efficient and capable but that she looked like a horrible old hag. But I've just seen her and she's about eighteen years old, extremely pretty and . . .'

'But she's *not* my secretary,' interrupted Mr. Smith, who had been thinking very rapidly. 'My secretary is ill today and so sent her grand-daughter to help out instead.'

SECRETS

550. My wife thinks that a secret is something you tell one person at a time.

SERVANTS

551. The new maid had just arrived to work at the magnificent stately pile in which live the Duke and Duchess.

'One thing is very important,' said the Duchess, imperiously, 'and that is that my husband and I always have breakfast at eight sharp.'

The new maid nodded her head in agreement and said: 'Sounds fine by me, Duchess. If I should sleep late, please feel free to start without me. I never eat much breakfast anyway.'

SHIPS

552. Passenger: 'Steward, can you telephone from a ship?'

Steward: 'Certainly, sir. A ship is something that floats in the water and carries passengers or cargo and a 'phone is something you can talk into and be heard miles away.'

SHOES

553. Customer: 'Do you have any crocodile shoes?'

Shoe shop assistant: 'Certainly, madam. What size feet do your crocodiles have?'

SHOPS

554. Shopping in a supermarket is a very educational process. Before I went there I didn't know that fish had ten fingers.

555. Customer: 'Can I have half a pound of mixed nuts, please?'

Shop assistant: 'Certainly, madam.'

Customer: 'And please make sure there are not too many coconuts.'

556. Mrs. Ponsonby-Smythe-Wigglehampton went to her local fishmongers and looked at the lobsters.

She prodded one of the lobsters and it started to crawl away. 'Hmm,' she said.

'They're beautiful lobsters, madam,' said the fishmonger. 'And, as you can see they're still alive.'

'I can see that,' said Mrs. Ponsonby-Smythe-Wigglehampton in a disdainful tone. 'But are they fresh?'

557. The man was in the Army Surplus store browsing around when a shop assistant came up to him and asked: 'Can I help you sir?'

'No thanks,' replied the man. 'I think I've found what I want.' And he selected an army penknife. 'It's a gift for my wife,' he explained.

'Is it going to be a surprise?' asked the shop assistant. 'If so, we can gift wrap it for you.'

'Yes, please,' said the man. 'That way it will also be a double surprise – she's expecting a diamond bracelet.'

558. Mrs. Bloggis: 'I'd like some nuts, please.'

Shop assistant: 'Certainly, madam. What sort?'

Mrs. Bloggis: 'Cashew.'

Shop assistant: 'Bless you! Now what nuts would you like, madam?'

SHOWER
559. 'Simon, did you take a shower this morning?'

'Why, mum, is it missing?'

SIGN LANGUAGE
560. The only language my wife uses when she goes shopping is sign language – she signs for everything.

SINGERS
561. Eva Screamalot was introduced at her latest concert by a compère who said: 'Our next singer almost didn't make it here tonight. After her last appearance she almost quit

because of her throat – the audience threatened to cut it.'

562. A friend of mine has such a remarkable singing voice he's just got a job on a luxury cruise liner – as the fog horn.

563. Godfrey went to audition as a singer at a small local club. The club pianist asked him: 'Can you read music?'

'Yes,' replied Godfrey, looking at a book in front of him, 'M.U.S.I.C.'

564. My young daughter's singing is rather like a quiz show – Maim That Tune.

565. Fred: 'What key do you sing in?'
Geoffrey: 'Chubb or Yale.'

SKUNKS
566. Tom: 'How many skunks do you need to make a really great stink?'
John: 'Quite a phew.'

SLEEP
567. Sally: 'How did you sleep last night?'
Debbie: 'Oh, just the same as always – with my eyes closed.'

568. Mother: 'Why have you dragged your bed out into the woodshed?'
Samantha: 'Because I want to sleep like a log.'

569. Sally: 'I don't think I'll be able to do much work today. I'm so sleepy! I didn't manage to get to sleep until after three.'
Samantha: 'I'm not surprised you're tired! One man – or two at the most – are enough for me. But three . . . ?'

SOLDIERS
570. Claude: 'When I grow up I want to be in the army.'
Mother: 'Why? You're only four now and I'm sure you'll change your mind as you get older.'

Claude: 'I won't change my mind. I want to be a soldier.'

Mother: 'But what if you get in a war and have to fight and get killed?'

Claude: 'But who would want to kill me?'

Mother: 'The enemy.'

Claude: 'That's all right, then. I'll be in the enemy army.'

SPEECHES

571. 'Why did you walk out in the middle of my speech?' demanded the company Chairman of one of his senior executives. 'It was a very important meeting of shareholders and you chose the most crucial moment to walk out when I had been speaking for only forty-five minutes.'

'I'm sorry, sir,' replied the senior executive, 'but it wasn't anything personal. I was just sleepwalking.'

SPORTS AND SOCIAL CLUB

572. Gerald: 'I understand the sports and social club is looking for a treasurer.'

Edwin: 'That's right.'

Gerald: 'But I thought the sports and social club only hired a treasurer a few months ago?'

Edwin: 'They did. That's the treasurer they are looking for.'

STRIP POKER

573. It has been said that strip poker is the only card game in which the more you lose, the more you have to show for it.

SUNDAY SCHOOL

574. Sunday School teacher: 'Now, Jonathan, can you tell me what sort of people go to Heaven?'

Jonathan: 'Dead ones, miss.'

SWORD SWALLOWERS

575. I once knew a sword swallower who swallowed an

umbrella. He said he wanted to put something away for a rainy day.

T

TAXIDERMY

576. The little old lady went to the taxidermist and took from her bag two large, but dead, cats.

'These poor creatures were mine,' she said. 'They were always so very much in love – Fred and Freda – and it almost broke my heart when they died. Can you stuff them in a lifelike manner?'

'Certainly, madam,' replied the taxidermist. 'Do you want them mounted?'

The little old lady thought for a moment, then shook her head sadly: 'I know they were very much in love, but I think it would be more – how shall I put it – delicate, if they were just holding paws instead.'

TELEPHONE CONVERSATIONS

577. Caller: 'Hello? Is that the Wigglesby residence?'

Fred Bloggis: 'No. I'm afraid it isn't.'

Caller: 'Oh! I must have dialled the wrong number. I'm sorry to have troubled you.'

Fred Bloggis: 'No trouble at all. The 'phone was ringing anyway.'

TELEVISION

578. The problem with American television detective/police series is not deciding which to watch but deciding which is which.

579. I thought the television programmes had improved tremendously – until my wife told me I'd been watching the fish tank she'd swapped for the TV.

THEATRE

580. Simon: 'I took my wife to the theatre last night – but we only saw the first Act and then had to leave.'

Sally: 'Why was that?'

Simon: 'Well, on the programme it said: "Act Two: Two days later" – and we couldn't stay in the theatre that long.'

581. The wealthy man booked the royal box at the London theatre so that he could take his pet elephant with him to watch a play.

Everyone was surprised at how well the elephant behaved and the manager of the theatre commented on this: 'Your elephant certainly seemed to enjoy himself. I could see him paying close attention to everything. I must say I was somewhat surprised that he should like the play so much.'

'So was I,' replied the wealthy man. 'When he read the book the play was based on he didn't like it at all.'

TOASTERS

582. Jeffrey: 'We have a Red Indian toaster at home.'

Jeremy: 'What's a Red Indian toaster?'

Jeffrey: 'Instead of the toast popping up it sends up smoke signals.'

TOILET WATER

583. The last time Tom's wife put toilet water behind her ears the seat fell on her.

TOMBSTONE

584. When Sally saw the tombstone with the inscription: 'Here lies the body of a politician and an honest man' she wondered how they managed to get two people into the same grave.

TRAIN JOURNEY

585. Two men were sitting together in the first class compartment of a train when one of them leaned forward and said: 'Haven't I seen your face somewhere else?'

The other man paused to reflect on the situation and then

said: 'No, I'm sorry. But my face has always been between my ears.'

TRAMPS
586. Within a few weeks of winning a fortune on the football pools, an elderly tramp died of a heart attack. In his will he decreed that most of his money was to be used for upholstering as many park benches as possible.

TRAVELS
587. Claire: 'I know something that travels all over the world but still remains in a corner?'
   Catherine: 'What?'
   Claire: 'A postage stamp.'

588. George: 'What are you going to do tomorrow?'
   Julia: 'I'm going to Bury St. Edmunds.'
   George: 'Oh! I didn't know he'd just died.'

TURTLES
589. Two small crabs were walking along the beach in Malaysia when one said to the other: 'I can't remember who my mother is.'

'That's terrible,' said the other crab. 'Maybe you should go and ask a turtle – they have tremendous memories.'

'Oh,' replied the first crab. 'I didn't know turtles had such good memories.'

'Of course,' commented the other crab. 'Haven't you heard of turtle recall?'

UPPER CRUST
590. Someone once defined the upper crust as being a hard-baked group of crumbs supported by a lot of dough.

U.S.S.R.

591. Jeremy was on a visit to the U.S.S.R. as a violinist with a British orchestra that was due to perform at a concert in Moscow.

Prior to the concert Jeremy strolled around Moscow and then sat in a park where he decided to study some of the music he was to play that night.

No sooner had he opened his sheet music than he was pounced on by KGB men and hauled off to be interrogated.

Jeremy denied doing anything illegal or subversive but the KGB continued their questioning for several days during which time Jeremy was kept in a small room and given only bread and water as sustenance. Then a KGB officer marched into the room and waved the sheet music at Jeremy.

'It is no good you denying that this is a code,' said the KGB officer. 'Handel has already confessed.'

V

VANITY

592. John: 'Would you say that I am very vain?'

Sarah: 'No, of course not. Why?'

John: 'Well, other men as handsome, intelligent and sexy as me usually are very vain.'

VENICE

593. A friend of mine went to Venice but left after a few hours as she said the streets were flooded.

VIDEO RECORDERS

594. Clarence: 'What would you like for Christmas?'

Clara: 'A video cassette recorder. But I know we can't afford one.'

Clarence: 'That's all right. I'll sell something in order to get enough money for one.'

Clara: 'What will you sell?'
Clarence: 'The television set.'

WAGES
595. Twenty years ago I used to dream about the time when I would be living in fantastic luxury on the same wages that are now keeping me below the poverty line.

WALKING
596. Sarah: 'Why are you walking like a crab?'
Jane: 'It's these new pills I'm taking – they have side effects.'

WAR BABY
597. My husband was a war baby. When he was born his parents took one look at him and started fighting.

WEATHER
598. Samantha: 'Is it freezing cold outside?'
Sally: 'I don't know. Everything is covered in snow.'

599. Sally: 'How did you find the weather on holiday?'
Debbie: 'I just went outside and there it was.'

WEDDING ANNIVERSARIES
600. In Hollywood when people celebrate their tenth wedding anniversary it means they're celebrating having been married ten times.

601. Mr. Jones: 'Darling, why have you given me this beautifully wrapped box containing these magnificent cufflinks? You are a thoughtful wife! They're just what I wanted.'

Mrs. Jones: 'Darling, surely you know why I gave them to you? It's your fifteenth wedding anniversary present.'

Mr. Jones: 'Oh! You must let me know when yours is, so that I can give you a present, too!'

602. Mr. and Mrs. Smith had been married fifty years but had always had many friends and so not missed never having any children.

The Golden Wedding Anniversary celebrations had been very successful and so it was a slightly drunk Mr. and Mrs. Smith who went to bed shortly after the last guest had left.

In bed, Mrs. Smith lay and looked at the ceiling as she said: 'You know, all this festivity brings back memories of our wedding.'

'And our honeymoon,' said Mr. Smith.

'Yes. It was a pity we were both so young and inexperienced then. Sixteen really was too young for people in those days to have got married. Of course, young people today know far more about the facts of life than we ever did when we first got married.'

'I know, dear,' replied Mr. Smith. 'Young people today wouldn't have had the same difficulties we had on our wedding night.'

'Darling,' said Mrs. Smith, 'would you like to try for a second time?'

WEDDINGS

603. If the bride wears white for her wedding as a symbol of purity and joy – then why does the groom always wear the opposite, black?

604. Freda and Albert had just got married in church and, with the ceremony over, Albert whispered to the clergyman: 'How much do I owe you?'

'Oh!' replied the clergyman. 'Talking about such earthly things as money always embarrasses me. Let's say you just give me what you think it is worth to have married Freda.'

Albert thought for a few moments and then handed the clergyman thirty-five pounds.

The clergyman looked at Freda, frowned, and then gave Albert thirty pounds back.

605. The young couple had a rough and ready wedding. The groom was rough and the bride was ready.

606. I recently went to a wedding which was the result of a love match pure and simple: the bride was pure and the groom was simple.

607. The groom turned to his best man as he finished signing the marriage register and said: 'Well, that's that! Now to go and collect a little bet.'

608. When thirty-eight stone Charles marries eighteen stone Melissa it will be the biggest wedding in town.

WEEVILS

609. The public health inspector was sent to Merseyside to look for the destructive beetle of the Curculionidae family known as the weevil.

The public health inspector dutifully searched in Liverpool and the surrounding areas – and even looked in the sea – but he finally had to report back to his boss in Liverpool: 'Here no weevil, sea no weevil, Speke no weevil.'

WELLINGTONS

610. Boring man, detailing at great length his war experiences: 'And I also flew Wellingtons.'

Bored young lady: 'And now you expect me to believe that wellington boots can fly?'

WILDLIFE

611. A friend of mine believes in preserving wildlife. So far he's already pickled six squirrels, five rabbits, two foxes, and a stoat.

WILD WEST

612. It was the time of the American Wild West and one day a party of soldiers rode out to find their tracker.

After riding for about an hour they found him, with his ear pressed firmly to the ground.

'Stage coach just pass by here,' mumbled the tracker.

'How do you know?' asked one of the soldiers.

'Because,' replied the tracker, 'it ran right over me.'

WILLS

613. In Henry's Will he instructs his wife to have him cremated and then send his ashes in a large buff envelope to the local tax inspector with a note stating: 'I hope you're now happy – you've got the lot!'

614. Paul's grandmother changed her Will six times – she was a fresh heir fiend.

WITCHES

615. Why do witches fly around on broomsticks?

Because vacuum cleaners are too noisy.

WIVES

616. When Henry told his wife he was feeling half dead she quickly picked him up, threw him over her shoulder and carried him to the local cemetery where she buried him up to his waist.

617. The only voice I get in what my wife purchases in the shops is the invoice.

618. Claude: 'How many wives have you had?'

Fred: 'About fifteen – but only one was my own.'

619. Ronald: 'All my wife says to me is "Money, money," she is always asking me for money.'

Roland: 'Why does she need so much? What does she spend it on?'

Ronald: 'I've no idea. I never give her any.'

620. One man I know hasn't spoken to his wife for ten years – he's far too polite to interrupt her talking.

621. I always know that if I come back from the office to a beautiful welcoming wife, with a delicious meal and fine wine on the table – I'm in the wrong house.

622. Cuthbert: 'I've got the best wife in the country.'
Clarence: 'You're lucky! Mine lives with me in London.'

623. My wife has a good sense of rumour.

624. Cuthbert's wife is so stupid she once rinsed some ice cubes in hot water and then spent an afternoon searching for where they went.

625. Everything my wife eats goes to waist.

626. Tom's wife has suffered considerably for her beliefs – the belief that she can get into size 10 dresses when she's size 14.

627. Fred: 'I call my wife a peach.'
John: 'That's nice. Is it because she's soft, sweet and juicy?'
Fred: 'No. It's because she's got a heart of stone.'

628. My wife has recently got a job that takes a lot of guts. She makes guitar strings.

629. Talk, talk, talk! That's all my wife ever does. I'm fed up! I've given her the best ears of my life.

630. Sally is the most sexy, adorable, intelligent wife in the whole world. Pity I'm married to Nora.

WOODPECKERS

631. A woodpecker was talking to a chicken. 'Woodpeckers are much cleverer than you chickens.'

'What makes you say that?' asked the chicken. 'You seem to spend all your day banging your head against a tree.'

'Ah!' responded the woodpecker. 'But have you ever heard of Kentucky Fried Woodpecker?'

WORK

632. Mr. Williams was angry with his son, who just seemed to laze about the house all day, even though he had been given a good education and was now twenty-two years old.

'You can't hang around waiting for a top job to come along,' said Mr. Williams. 'You've got to start somewhere. Why don't you do the same as I did? Start as a humble accounts clerk. Within five years I'd made enough to start my own business.'

'I know, Dad,' replied the son, 'but that's not possible these days – they have proper auditors now!'

Y

YEAST

633. A friend of mine eats yeast and shoe polish before going to bed – he likes to rise and shine.

Z

ZOO

634. Amelia recently got forcibly ejected from the zoo because she fed the rabbits. She fed them to the tigers.

635. I hear that at the local zoo they are trying to cross a carrier pigeon with a woodpecker: they are aiming to breed a bird that will not only deliver messages but also knock first.

Readers may be interested in the wide range of Paperfronts available. A full catalogue can be had by sending S.A.E. to the address below.

ELLIOT RIGHT WAY BOOKS, KINGSWOOD, SURREY, U.K.